THE 1980'S:
COUNTDOWN
TO
ARMAGEDDON

THE 1980'S: COUNTDOWN TO ARMAGEDDON

BY HAL LINDSEY

Lakeland
Marshall Morgan & Scott
3 Beggarwood Lane, Basingstoke, Hants., UK

Copyright © 1980 by 'The Aorist Corporation, Inc.'
First published in the U.S.A. 1981 by Bantam Books, Inc.,
666 Fifth Avenue, New York, New York 10103.
First published in the UK by Marshall Morgan & Scott 1983

ISBN 0 551 01073 8

Reproduced, printed and bound in Great Britain by
Hazell Watson & Viney Ltd, Aylesbury, Bucks

Dedication

To Steve Scott, without whose vision and encouragement this book wouldn't have been started, much less finished.

To Bob Marsh, whose faith helped me become what he believed me to be.

Acknowledgment

I wish to give special praise to my editor, Bill Tonelli, whose skill helped immensely in the preparation of this book.

CONTENTS

What On Earth Is Happening? / **xi**

CHAPTER ONE
Some Pleasant Surprises / **1**

CHAPTER TWO
A Look at the Prophetic Scenario / **9**

CHAPTER THREE
Birth Pains / **17**

CHAPTER FOUR
Up Against the Wall / **35**

CHAPTER FIVE
The Crescent of Crisis / **51**

CHAPTER SIX
The Bear Moves Southward / **65**

CHAPTER SEVEN
Kings of the East / **87**

CHAPTER EIGHT
The Roman Empire—Phase II / **97**

CHAPTER NINE
The New World System / **115**

CHAPTER TEN
What About the U.S.? / **129**

CHAPTER ELEVEN
Lesson From a Fig Tree / **159**

Footnotes / **177**

WHAT ON EARTH IS HAPPENING?

• U.S. stages unsuccessful attempt to rescue embassy hostages in Iran. NATO nations and other allies are *angered* by America's military try to free its citizens.

• A communist rebel is elected president of Zimbabwe (formerly Rhodesia).

• Three highly-esteemed Rabbis, members of Israel's ultra-orthodox community, each have identical dreams— dreams that depict the imminent coming of the Messiah.

• Russia ignores five U.S. warnings and invades Afghanistan, committing various atrocities including the use of nerve gas.

• The Carter Administration approves the sale of sophisticated technology and military hardware to Red China.

• For the first time in history, Israel and Egypt establish diplomatic relations.

• Inflation rate in the U.S. soars, nearing 20 percent a year.

• Russia refuses to withdraw combat troops from Cuba, and instead conducts battle manuevers there.

• Israel discovers oil in the Dead Sea region captured during the Six-Day War.

• The European Common Market accepts its 10th member and elects a parliament

• Carter Administration vows to get the SALT II treaty ratified by Congress, despite renewed Soviet aggression.

• U.S. government severely restricts CIA and FBI operations; meanwhile, the Soviet KGB enjoys great freedom, employing 300 agents at the United Nations alone.

- The government of Liberia is toppled by a military coup.

- Israel angers the Arab world by confiscating additional Arab-owned property.

- Sweden outlaws disciplining children; in the U.S., children successfully sue their parents for a kind of "malpractice."

- Russia amasses 1 million troops along the Soviet-China border.

- Western Europe, Egypt, Israel and the Arab nations are enraged by a U.S. vote mixup at the United Nations.

- A U.S. Congressman reveals that only half of the U.S. fighter plane force can fly at any given time due to lack of spare parts and maintenance.

- Pentagon official warns that Russia could conquer the Persian Gulf, and the U.S. couldn't stop it—without using nuclear weapons.

- Air Force experts say U.S. air defenses are so porous that as many as 50 Soviet bombers could sneak through the radar "net" and surprise key command centers.

- U.S. cancels all bomber plane production, while the U.S.S.R. builds a new supersonic bomber every 12 days.

These are but a few of the current events causing tremendous interest and concern among students of the ancient Hebrew prophets. How these events fit into the prophetic pattern and what they point to for the future are the subjects of this book.

If the events detailed in this book were examined independently, it would be easy to miss their significance regarding the picture of the future painted by the Hebrew prophets.

However, when each is considered in light of all the others, one thing becomes obvious: We are moving at an ever-accelerating rate of speed into a prophetic countdown. The very destiny of mankind is at stake.

ONE
SOME PLEASANT SURPRISES

I had been asleep for several hours when the phone rang. Startled and still half asleep, I fumbled around for the receiver and clicked on the lamp. While my eyes tried to focus on the bedside clock, I heard a distant and unfamiliar voice ask in a proper British accent, "Are you the Hal Lindsey who wrote that book on prophecy?"

I cautiously answered yes, and my caller began telling me about the impact *The Late Great Planet Earth* had made upon his life and the lives of many of his acquaintances. The gentleman said he was a prominent attorney and was active in the government of his country, Jamaica. He had passed out about 1,500 copies of the book to his friends and fellow government officials.

He told me how he, along with many others, had come to believe the message of the book, and he asked if I would come to Jamaica to tell them what they should do next. I caught the first available flight.

When I arrived in Jamaica, I was surprised to find several hundred people gathered to hear what the Bible's prophets had to say about current events and our immediate future.

3

A NEW PROPHETIC PHENOMENON

Shortly after *The Late Great Planet Earth* was published I began to see a most unusual phenomenon taking place. People from all walks of life were becoming captivated by an intense interest in the relevancy of the predictions made by the Hebrew prophets thousands of years ago.

This interest wasn't confined to religious people, either. It extended all the way from college students to scientists to government officials both here and abroad.

The interest also proved to have no geographical boundaries, as the book was translated into 31 foreign editions which were circulated in more than 50 countries. I began receiving letters and even phone calls literally from around the world.

AN ISRAELI PILOT

While attending a Christmas reception at the home of a friend, Dan McKinnon, a newspaper publisher and radio station owner, I was introduced to one of the greatest fighter pilots alive today. Dan met this handsome young Israeli while writing an article on fighter pilots taking advanced training at the Miramar Naval Air Station outside of San Diego.

In my book I had written a great deal about Israel, expressing my love for the Israeli people and my concern for their survival. Dan knew this and rightly assumed that I would be interested in meeting this pilot. He also felt that the pilot would want to talk with me, since my book had shown that the prophecies relevant to our times were centered on Israel and its future.

Dan introduced us, and we talked for quite some time. Later, he and I became close friends. Before we parted that night, I gave the young pilot a copy of *Late Great*, and he read it from cover to cover.

Later this man told me that while he couldn't agree with some of the points in the book, he believed the passages concerning the Middle East and its future to be absolutely true. He said that having fought for Israel nearly all his life, he had seen the very things the book dealt with taking place. He was amazed to discover that these events had been so precisely foretold thousands of years ago by his own people's prophets.

A short time later I heard from this pilot again. He was back in the U.S., attending the American Air War College, an Air Force school that teaches air warfare strategy to military commanders. My friend asked the school's commanding general for permission to invite me to speak there on the military aspects of Bible prophecy as they relate to the Middle East and World War III.

I guess the general was so amazed to hear an Israeli request a speaker on Biblical prophets that he approved my talk. Even though attendance was totally voluntary, virtually the entire school turned out, including many officers accompanied by their wives.

At the meeting I simply set forth what the prophets Daniel, Ezekiel and Zachariah had forecast, as well as the predictions of the other Hebrew prophets. I outlined the spheres of political power that would come together in the last days and showed how Israel would be the focal point of all the conflicts, igniting the last war of the world. To my surprise, the audience responded to the message with an enthusiastic ovation.

MEANWHILE, AT THE PENTAGON . . .

One year later I was invited to speak at the Pentagon. It seems that a number of officers and non-military personnel alike had read *Late Great* and wanted to hear more.

A meeting was set and when I arrived I was amazed to find hundreds of people jamming the room. Outside, others were trying to crowd in. All of these people wanted to hear what the prophets had to say about our destiny. When I finished, the response was overwhelming.

After my talk, one officer told me that various Pentagon officials had independently come to the same conclusions I had reached regarding the future of the Middle East. They had reached those same conclusions with virtually no knowledge of what the Hebrew prophets had predicted 2,000 to 3,000 years earlier.

COMPUTER CONFIRMATION

On another occasion I was invited to speak at a home in an exclusive suburb overlooking Los Angeles. When I entered the house I was greeted by a group of very distinguished-looking men. I had no idea of who they were or what they did.

As I spoke about the detailed accounts of how the final world war would develop, as recorded in Daniel, chapter 11, verses 40–45, I was impressed by the total attention they were paying to what I said. I continued and discussed the forces that would be involved in the war, the way the troops would move, the battles that would take place and how the war would spread to the rest of the world. I noticed that the men were visibly moved by what I said.

When I ended my talk, I learned that my audience was part of an elite group charged with an awesome responsibility. Their job—I cannot reveal who they worked for—was to gather the latest military intelligence on every nation's war-making potential, decide what America's response should be and then predict the final outcome of any conflicts. They used sophisticated computers to perform these tasks.

A few days before our meeting, their computer had predicted the same events and outcomes that had been forecast by Daniel. Needless to say, they were more surprised by Daniel's words than I was by theirs.

THE ISRAELI REACTION

On numerous occasions I have been asked how Israel has responded to *The Late Great Planet Earth*. It's true, it is difficult for books with New Testament overtones to gain acceptance in Israel.

In 1971, I accompanied a newspaper reporter on a fact-finding tour of Israel sponsored by the U.S. Department of State. Early in the tour I met a major assigned to Israeli army intelligence. This officer, an attractive woman, served as our interpreter and became a good friend.

After the major read my book she urged that it be translated into Hebrew. My publisher contacted an Israeli book firm, and a Hebrew edition was soon available. My major friend helped with the translation, using modern-day Israeli vernacular that made the book even more readable.

As a result of her work, the book caught on like wildfire. A great many copies circulated among military men and government officials as well.

A NEW URGENCY

Ever since *The Late Great Planet Earth* I have thought about writing another book on how prophecy relates to current events. But only recently have I felt compelled to do so. So many of the things which have occurred during the past 10 years are so directly related to prophecy that I now sense an urgent, even a desperate compulsion to bring readers up to date.

The goal of this book is not merely to show which prophecies have been fulfilled since *Late Great* came out in 1970, however. Even more important, it is intended to analyze what will occur in the decade we have just entered.

During the 25 years I have been studying prophecy I have seen incredible events forecast 3,000 years ago happen right before my eyes. Especially in the past 10 years, I have watched current events push us toward the climax of history the prophets foretold. I believe many people will be shocked by what is happening right now and by what will happen in the very near future. *The decade of the 1980's could very well be the last decade of history as we know it.*

TWO
A LOOK AT THE PROPHETIC SCENARIO

"The Bible gives a ratio of forces at a given political situation of the end times which, if read in the context of today, does begin to look familiar."

—Major General Chaim Herzog,
Israeli ambassador to the U.N.

The Hebrew prophets began predicting the pattern of future world events thousands of years ago. By A.D. 95, the Bible's forecast for the last days was set down in the pages of the Apocalypse, also known as the Book of Revelation.

Ten years ago, *The Late Great Planet Earth* spelled out how the world's spheres of power would combine and collide in the final stage of history. For the more than 30 million who read that book, this chapter will serve as a review. For those of you who haven't read it, what follows here will be a necessary introduction to the prophecies concerning our times. For more details, read *The Late Great Planet Earth*.

THE REBIRTH OF ISRAEL

The center of the entire prophetic forecast is the State of Israel. Certain events in that nation's recent history prove the accuracy of the prophets. They also force us to accept the fact that the "countdown" has begun.

Thirty-five hundred years ago, Moses predicted that the Jewish nation would be destroyed. He said the Jews would

11

be scattered throughout the world and would have no assurance of life. Fear, Moses said, would stalk them day and night (Deuteronomy 28:63–68). He also predicted that just before the end of this present age, the Jews would return to their homeland and form their nation once again.

Other prophets, including Ezekiel, Zachariah, Daniel and Micah went into great detail about the rebirth of Israel. Ezekiel, in chapters 36 through 38, said the Hebrew survivors would return to Palestine, be miraculously reborn as a nation and prosper.

As Moses predicted, the Jewish nation was destroyed. And after nearly 2,000 years of wandering through exile, the Jews returned to Palestine and formed the nation of Israel on May 14, 1948. On that day, the prophetic countdown began!

Many skeptics point out that during World Wars I and II, some well-meaning students of prophecy claimed that the end of history was at hand and the Messiah would return soon.

Some of these students proclaimed Hitler the anti-Christ and Italian dictator Benito Mussolini the false prophet described in the prophecies. Naturally, when the world didn't end, all prophecy was discredited.

These skeptics have asked me, "Why do you think that all the various prophecies will come to pass during *this* generation?"

The answer is simple. The prophets told us that the rebirth of Israel—no other event—would be the sign that the countdown had begun. Since that rebirth, the rest of the prophecies have begun to be fulfilled quite rapidly. For this reason I am convinced that we are now in the unique time so clearly and precisely forecast by the Hebrew prophets.

THE ARAB-MOSLEM CONFEDERACY

The second piece of the prophetic puzzle concerns the Arab nations. The prophets said that the Arabs, fragmented for so many centuries, would become united in the last days. The basis for their unity would be their common desire to destroy the newly-formed nation of Israel.

Certainly, even the most casual observer of the Middle East situation must recognize the unprecedented unification of the Arabs over the past 30 years.

THE RISE OF THE SOVIET UNION

The third part of the scenario predicts the rise of the greatest military power the world has ever known. Ezekiel, Daniel and Zachariah all said that a nation to the extreme north of Israel would achieve great influence and become a threat to the whole world. They said this power would be Israel's mortal enemy.

The prophets predicted that this nation would launch an all-out land and sea attack on Israel, the Arab nations and the continent of Africa.

This country, Bible scholars agree, is the Soviet Union. A line drawn due north of Israel crosses only one land mass— Russia. And the three tribes Ezekiel predicted would people the nation to the north are in fact the ancestors of today's Russians.

Throughout its history, the single most consistent motive of the Soviet Union's military invasions has been the acquisition of warm-water ports for its merchant and naval fleets. Recently, the importance of oil has made the Persian Gulf and the Middle East even more attractive to the Russians.

In *The Late Great Planet Earth* I predicted that the Soviets would begin their Middle East campaign with a sweep through the Persian Gulf area into Iran. The recent Russian invasion of Afghanistan was a first step in that direction. Once the Middle East falls to Russia, the communists will withhold their newly-gained oil to cripple the west. Just how close the Soviets are to making this bold move will be discussed in a later chapter.

THE RISE OF RED CHINA

The fourth part of the pattern involves the Orient. A power known in the Bible as the "Kings of the East" will move an army of 200 million soldiers into the Soviet-Middle East war, the prophets and the Book of Revelation say.

Remember, this troop number was predicted at a time when the greatest armies in the world only numbered in the tens of thousands. In fact, not only was 200 million soldiers a preposterous number for an army, but the *total population of the world* was only a fraction of 200 million at that time.

The Chinese will spread the war to the rest of the world. Every major city will be leveled and more than half the world's population will die during the ensuing battles.

As far back as 1961, China's leaders boasted they could mobilize an amy of 200 million soldiers. Most Bible scholars agree that the "Kings of the East" represents China and its Asian allies.

THE REVIVAL OF THE ROMAN EMPIRE

The final piece of the scenario the Bible forecasts is the return of the Roman Empire in the form of a 10-nation confederacy.

This confederacy will begin as a trade and economic organization. But once it is firmly established, a world political leader will rise from its ranks. This man will have powers of persuasion that no one in the troubled world of the future will be able to resist.

This man will be viewed as a kind of "secular savior." He will reveal brilliant plans for solving the Middle East crisis, ending war, helping the world's impoverished nations and so on.

Of course, this man is the anti-Christ the prophets heralded. Aided by Satan, he will lead humanity down the path to utter destruction.

As I wrote 10 years ago in *The Late Great Planet Earth*, I believe this man is alive today—alive and waiting to come forth.

When I wrote that in *Late Great*, the only possible successor to the Roman Empire (in my opinion) was the European Common Market. But a decade ago, that organization had just six member nations, not the 10 the Bible forecast.

In 1979, Greece became the 10th member of the Common Market.

Recently, the Common Market went beyond its original economic and trade functions and elected a parliament. This move will eventually fulfill the Common Market's long-range goal—to unify its members into a single political body.

The Common Market is disillusioned with the U.S. The early 1980 fiasco of the United Nations vote on Israel's rights in East Jerusalem demonstrated to the European nations that the U.S. is not a reliable ally. Events such as the U.N. vote, which increase tensions throughout the world, will bind this European confederacy more tightly in the future.

Thus we have all five pieces of the prophets' scenario for the later days. All the powers—Israel, the Arabs, Russia, China and the revived Roman Empire—are fixed in place.

Now let's examine what has happened throughout the world during the past decade and see how these events will lead us to the climax of history.

THREE
BIRTH PAINS

"I think human life is threatened as never before in the history of this planet. Not just by one peril, but by many perils that are all working together and coming to a head at about the same time. And that time lies very close to the year 2000. I am one of those scientists who finds it hard to see how the human race is to bring itself much past the year 2000."

—Dr. George Wald,
Nobel Prize-winning scientist,
Harvard University

I'll never forget how puzzled I was the first few times I read Jesus's predictions of the signs which would herald the world's last great holocaust.

In the Bible, He told us that seven signals—war, revolution, plague, famine, earthquakes, religious deception and strange occurances in space—would alert us that the end of the old world and the birth of the new was near.

There has to be more to it, I thought. The phenomena He predicted just didn't seem all that phenomenal to me. After all, we've always had the "nations rising against nations" and "wars and rumor of war" He foretold. And earthquakes, famines, plagues—they've always been with us too. So how could we view any of these as signs that the final awesome event of the ages was about to begin?

Then one day, as I was reading the original Greek text of Matthew 24:8, it struck me. In the King James version of the Bible, Jesus ends His predictions this way: "All of these things are the beginning of sorrows."

But in the Greek it reads: "All of these things are the beginning of birth pains" (the New American Standard Bible and the New International Version both agree). Not "sorrows," Jesus said, but "birth pains."

LIGHT FROM NERVOUS FATHERS

That difference in translation led me to think about a woman's experience during labor. I saw the image of the nervous first-time father anxiously timing the space between his wife's painful contractions to determine the nearness of birth. The pain itself is not his signal: Only when the pains become more frequent and more intense does he know that the baby is about to be born.

And there was my clue! The mere presence of the seven conditions forecast by Jesus was not the sign we were to watch for. Only as these conditions, these "birth pains," became more frequent and more intense would we know that the final days of our suffering—and the birth of the new world—were upon us.

Over the past 10 years the appearance of Jesus's signs has accelerated, and today, we find them occurring one on top of the other. Let me report on the signs I see and maybe we can learn what is in store for us.

BIRTH PAIN NO. 1: RELIGIOUS DECEPTION

The movement of major denominational Christian ministers away from their historic beliefs has become a stampede. There have been some hopeful sparks of life here and there, but mostly we see the basic historic doctrines of the Bible being tossed aside by church hierarchies both here and abroad.

The Bible warned of this. "For the time will come when men will not put up with sound doctrine. Instead, to suit their own desires, they will gather around them a great number of teachers to say what their itching ears want to hear. They will turn their ears from the truth and turn aside to myths."

The False Messiahs

Jesus said: "Watch out that no one deceives you. For many will come in my name, claiming 'I am the Messiah,' and will deceive many" (Matthew 24:4–5).

How many men claiming to be Christ or the Messiah have raised their voices over the past 10 years?

Maharaj Ji of India made this claim and gathered many followers. "The Lord from Heaven in a 747," he sometimes called himself.

Sun Myung Moon, a Korean, was also able to fill American stadiums with his believers. His disciples proclaimed him to be, among other things, the second coming of Christ.

David Moses, leader of the group known as the "Children of God," was another who attracted a large following, especially among young people. In his messages (nicknamed "Mo Letters") to his so-called "families" of adoring disciples, Moses too claimed Messianic authority.

History's most chilling encounter with a counterfeit Christ also came in the '70s, in the form of the Rev. Jim Jones. If his loyal followers had only checked Jones's teachings against those found in the Bible! Had the 900-plus men, women and children who perished in Jones's "communion of death" in the jungles of Guyana only known what Jesus had to say about false messiahs, their awful fate could have been avoided.

The Occult Revival

One of the many fads of the 1960's was an interest in the occult. But rather than fade away, as most fads do, belief in occultism has grown to the point where the average person today accepts occult and psychic phenomena as fact.

Well-educated professional people can be found taking part in seances, witchcraft, fortune telling, psychic healing and astrology. Police departments have even used "mediums" to help them solve tough cases.

Belief in the occult would not have endured beyond the fad

stage were it not for the sometimes startling phenomena which have accompanied this mysticism.

But we must remember this: Not all supernatural phenomena is good. There are actual malevolent spirits which can cause "miracles" of sorts to lead people away from truth and into deception.

Jesus predicted this fascination with the occult when He said: "For false messiahs and false prophets will appear and perform great signs and miracles to deceive even the elect (true believers)—if that were possible" (Matthew 24:24).

Elsewhere, the Bible relates this occult revival to our times in particular when it says: "The Spirit clearly says that in the later times some will abandon the faith and follow deceiving spirits and things taught by demons" (1 Timothy 4:1 NIB).

Early in the '70s, the movie "The Exorcist" started a whole trend in filmmaking which dealt with demonic possession. Movie-goers flocked to see these films for their fright value, just as movie-goers viewed films such as "Dracula" and "Frankenstein" decades earlier.

But I can testify that demonic possession—unlike movie monsters—is real and desperately dangerous. I have witnessed demonic possession and have been involved in some very real and sobering exorcisms.

BIRTH PAIN NO. 2: INTERNATIONAL REVOLUTION

"Nation will rise against nation, and kingdom against kingdom," Jesus predicted.

Jesus was talking about a time of political chaos, when nations would be ripped apart by civil war and revolution.

Today, we find many of the world's nations ruled by leaders who incite racial, religious and tribal strife within their own countries and in other countries as well. Recent histories of Africa, southeast Asia, the Middle East and Latin America will bear this out.

War in the name of "liberation" has also swept through parts of the world, backed by soldiers, arms and money from the major communist powers. This turbulent atmosphere has caused a breakdown in international law as well, as illustrated by the takeover of the U.S. embassy in Iran by armed terrorists.

Not a year goes by without at least one nation's government being overthrown.

BIRTH PAIN NO. 3: WAR

"And you will hear of wars and rumors of war . . ." (Matthew 24:6).

From the beginning of history, whether recorded in newspapers or ancient scrolls or on cave walls, we have heard the news of war being waged, constantly and continually.

But no period has witnessed the escalation of the weapons—and the stakes—of war as has the 20th century.

In our innocence, we dubbed the first major war of the century "The Great War." The "war to end all wars," we called it.

Then Hitler invaded Poland in 1939, and the second "great war" was on. Only then had we learned to begin numbering the times our entire planet was at war.

The carnage of World War II—about 60 million dead—paled, however, next to the event which ended that struggle.

The Japanese armies and citizens were prepared to die defending their islands. Our military leaders estimated that it would cost more than 1 million Allied army lives to end the conflict by traditional warfare.

So in August of 1945, the most terrible weapon known to that world, the atomic bomb, was unleashed on two Japanese cities, Hiroshima and Nagasaki. The death and destruction the bombs caused were like nothing before in history. Most likely, nothing less than the atomic bomb would have convinced the Japanese to surrender. Finally, they did just that.

On Sept. 2, 1945, aboard the U.S. Battleship Missouri, the formal papers of surrender were signed. After that brief ceremony, the world listened for the remarks by the supreme commander of the Allied force in the Pacific, General Douglas MacArthur.

An Unheeded Warning

As could be expected, part of MacArthur's address served as the closing note to a devastating conflict.

But he had more than that to say. We heard the conquering hero thunder forth a warning about the terrible new age of warfare the atomic blast had drawn us into.

Listen to his words: "A new era is upon us . . . The utter destruction of the war potential, through progressive advances in scientific discovery, has in fact now reached a point which revises the traditional concept of war.

"Men since the beginning of time have sought peace . . . military alliances, balances of power, leagues of nations all in turn failed, leaving the only path to be by way of the crucible of war.

"We have had our last chance. If we do not now devise some greater and more equitable system, Armageddon will be at our door."[1]

Battle Upon Battle

Three years after MacArthur's solemn warning, war broke out in the Middle East, spurred by the establishment of the state of Israel. Also in that year the "Cold War" between the U.S. and Russia broke out over the Soviet blockade of Berlin.

Two years later, the Korean war began to rage.

Israel returned to war in 1956, 1967 and 1973.

America's own deadly battle in Vietnam lingered on for eight years.

And as this book is written, the Russians have again shown the seriousness of their plan to dominate the world by invading Afghanistan (more on this later).

Recently, a special committee made up of representatives of the Massachusetts Institute of Technology and Harvard University was appointed by the U.S. government. The committee's job was to study the possibility of a major war breaking out in the near future.

The report stated that a limited nuclear war would probably be fought before 1984, and that an all-out nuclear holocaust appeared certain to occur before the end of the '90s.

If that confrontation is indeed "all out," what are our chances for survival? We have none, it seems. The world's superpowers now have enough nuclear ammunition to wipe out the entire human race.

WW II—In A Single Blast

The Russians, for instance, now arm some of their intercontinental missiles with 100-megaton nuclear warheads, says scientist Arthur Crawford.

It's difficult to imagine the power these missiles possess. So consider this: Just one of these warheads has more destructive power than all the bombs dropped by both sides in World War II.

If one of these warheads exploded over the state of Ohio, every living thing in that state would die. People looking in the direction of the blast from as far as 300 miles away would have their eyes burned out before they had a chance to turn their heads.

Poisonous radiation would continue to kill far beyond the range of the blast itself. And the state would be uninhabitable for centuries.

These 100-megaton warheads are now hidden in Soviet missile silos, aimed at U.S. population centers.

Jesus warned us in the Bible that in the last days of the world, man would destroy nearly everything that lives (Matthew 24:21–22). Now, for the first time in history, we have the potential to fulfill this prophecy.

BIRTH PAIN NO. 4: FAMINES

Jesus said, ". . . and in various places there will be famines" (Matthew 24:7)

In 1969, when I wrote *The Late Great Planet Earth*, many experts were warning of approaching widespread famines. People like Dr. Paul Erlich (author of *The Population Bomb*), Dr. Barry Commoner, a noted environmentalist and author, and Dr. William Paddock (author of *Famines 1975*) even went so far as to predict an "Age of Famines" beginning in the mid-1970's.

These experts used simple arithmetic to back their claims. Here are the most commonly-quoted figures: It took man from the beginning of time until the year A.D. 1850 to reach the first billion in population. It took from 1850 to 1930 to reach the 2 billion mark. It took from 1930 to 1960 to hit the third billion. And it only took from 1960 to 1975 to reach the fourth billion. Now we are really generating.

Today, in 1980, we are beyond the 4.5-billion mark and still going. Most authorities agree that we will double the 1975 population by the year 2000.

How will we feed all those people? We won't. In fact, we are nearing the point where there will not be enough food to keep us all alive.

Many experts say the age of famines began in 1974. In that year, terrible shortages broke out in parts of Africa and Asia. Even when emergency food supplies were sent, the starving millions didn't receive them in time.

That occurred because the feuding and inept governments either refused to admit there was a problem (as happened in Ethiopia) or they simply couldn't transport the food to the backward and underdeveloped regions where famines raged.

Worse yet was the situation in Cambodia. In 1979, hundreds of thousands starved to death there because the communist government refused—for "political reasons"—to distribute emergency food supplies to them. Food sent from other nations to feed the hungry was simply confiscated and turned over to the army.

Experts agree that famines will continue to happen, for the following reasons:

The Population Explosion

In the very countries least able to feed themselves, we find the greatest increases in population. Because of racial tradition and religious rules, many of these starving nations will not accept any type of birth control.

Oil Price Increases

For Americans, oil price increases meant some inconvenience. For those in the "famine zones," they meant death.

Oil is necessary to produce the larger crops made possible by the so-called "Green Revolution." This "revolution" centered around new technology which produced superstrains of grain which yielded more food. The only problem was that this technology required cheap petroleum for fertilizers and insecticides, in addition to oil needed to run farm machinery.

So when the oil producers quadrupled the price of their product in 1973, they literally guaranteed that millions of people in overpopulated, underdeveloped nations would starve.

Besides making it impossible for these people to farm their own land, the rise in the price of oil increased the cost of imported grain.

Because of the scarcity of oil at affordable prices, the father of the Green Revolution, Dr. Norman Borlaug, has declared that his revolution has failed.

Pollution

The overwhelming impact of industrial pollution upon our air, water and soil threatens both the quality and the quantity of our food. Scientists have demonstrated that foods today do not yield the same nutritional value that they did 30 years ago.

Changing Weather Patterns

California's bountiful San Joaquin Valley has been hit by "acid rains" in recent years. This phenomenon is caused by air pollution, which affects the clouds. According to a Los Angeles *Times* article, these strange rains are very harmful to the crops.

Just when we need to cultivate more land and produce more food another unexpected threat has appeared: Widespread changing weather patterns.

In an interview for a film documentary based on *The Late Great Planet Earth*, Dr. Borlaug said, "The changing picture on weather around the world is another variable that affects food production. There are many in the field of climatology who now say that the world's weather is changing."

Dr. John R. Gribbin, scientist and co-author of *The Jupiter Effect*, also predicts drastic changes in the world's weather, due to shifting planet orbits.

"The idea that the sun affects the climate patterns on Earth came to our attention through the study of earthquakes," Dr. Gribbin said.

"The unusual planetary alignment due to occur in the early 1980's will affect the sun. This in turn shakes up planet Earth. But we realized while studying the repercussions in the area of earthquakes that the link works through the atmosphere. What we are really talking about is an effect of the sun on the circulation of the atmosphere. And this determines weather pattern shifts."

So according to the best-informed experts, we will have less food just when we need more food than ever. Many people naively expect science to work some kind of miracle at the last minute.

But listen to the solemn warning of the greatest living expert in the field of food production, Dr. Borlaug. He said, "I think it's folly to expect science to pull a rabbit out of a hat in the 11th hour to solve the food production problem."

In our film interview, Dr. Borlaug said he believes "the hunger and misery of millions would provoke a great global holocaust."

BIRTH PAIN NO. 5:
EARTHQUAKES

Jesus foretold, ". . . in various places there will be earthquakes" (Matthew 24:7).

Earthquakes are a frightful phenomenon. Science knows how they happen, and something of why they happen, but little is known of when they will happen.

There have been many great earthquakes throughout history, but, according to surprisingly well-kept records, in the past they did not occur very frequently. The 20th century, however, has experienced an unprecedented increase in the frequency of these calamities. In fact, the number of earthquakes per decade has roughly doubled in each of the 10-year periods since 1950.

The Jupiter Effect

Dr. John R. Gribbin and Dr. Stephen H. Plagemann, authors of *The Jupiter Effect*, have predicted that history's greatest outbreak of earthquakes will occur around 1982. They make this claim because of an unusual astronomical phenomenon that occurs every 179 years. That phenomenon has been dubbed "the Jupiter effect."

The term describes a situation in which all of the planets of our solar system become aligned in a straight line perpendicular to the sun. This alignment causes great storms on the sun's surface, which in turn affect each of the planets.

The sun storms will not only affect our atmosphere, as was previously mentioned, but they will slow down the Earth's axis slightly. According to the book's authors, this slowing puts a tremendous strain on the Earth's faults, touching off earthquakes.

I can hear you asking, "Why will more earthquakes occur during 1982's version of the Jupiter Effect than happened in previous times?"

Scientists say that is because the construction of dams over fault lines weakens the Earth and causes more catastrophic quakes.

According to our author-experts, some of the scary side-effects of the new wave of quakes will be great floods—when dams built over faults are destroyed—and nuclear power plant meltdowns at facilities built on or near the Earth's faults.

The '70s: A Period of Increasing Quakes

The 1970's experienced the largest increase in the number of killer quakes known to history. In fact, the dramatic increase in quakes in 1976 led many scientists to say we are entering a period of great seismic disturbances.

The list of terrible tragedies in exhibit I underscores the coming fulfillment of Jesus's predictions. The new wave of quakes indicates that we are well on the way to the final stages of the prophetic timetable.

BIRTH PAIN NO. 6:
PLAGUES

Jesus predicted an increase in plagues during the final days (Luke 21:11).

In this day of modern medical science, plagues seem to be things of the past. But there are new factors which make plagues a real possibility for the future.

Part of the problem has to do with a previous "birth pain," famine. As the number of starving people grows, the chance for disease to spread increases. Today, more than half the

EXHIBIT I
MAJOR KILLER
EARTHQUAKES OF THE 1970'S

Year	Location	Toll
1970	Kutahya, Turkey	More than 1,000 dead
	Peru (northern)	More than 30,000 dead
1971	Los Angeles area	64 dead
	Bingol, Turkey	More than 800 dead
1972	Iran	45 villages leveled; more than 5,000 dead
	Managua, Nicaragua	70% of the city destroyed; more than 10,000 dead
1973	Mexico (central)	20,000 left homeless; 527 dead
1975	Lice, Turkey	3,372 injured; 2,312 dead
1976	Guatemala	1 million left homeless; 74,105 injured; 22,419 dead
	Italy (northeast)	More than 1,000 dead
	Indonesia	3,000 missing; 443 dead
	Bali, Indonesia	3,400 injured; 600 dead
	Tangshan, China (two quakes)	More than 700,000 dead; 2d worst disaster in history
	Philippines (south)	8,000 dead or missing
	Van province, Turkey	More than 4,000 dead
1977	Bucharest, Romania	11,275 injured; 1,541 dead
	Iran	520 dead
1978	Tobas, Iran	More than 25,000 dead
1979	Iran (eastern)	199 dead
	Yugoslavia	80,000 left homeless; 1,500 injured; 129 dead

world's population gets less than the minimum nutrition needed to live in good health.

This overpopulation in the world's poorest regions also causes sanitation problems. Combined with shortages of medicine and doctors, this is turning these poor areas into breeding grounds for disease.

BIRTH PAIN NO. 7:
STRANGE EVENTS IN THE SKIES

"There will be terrors and great signs from heaven," Jesus forecasts for the last days (Luke 21:11 NASB).

The Greek word for "sign" means a supernatural phenomenon intended to point its observer to a profound truth.

The Greek word for heaven can mean three things—the atmosphere around the Earth, outer space or the place where God dwells.

I believe Jesus meant the word "heaven" to take the first two possibilities, the skies and beyond. He went on to say: "There will be signs in the sun, moon and stars. On the Earth, nations (Gentiles) will be in anguish and perplexity at the roaring and tossing of the sea. Men will faint from terror, apprehensive of what is coming to the world, for the heavenly bodies will be shaken" (Luke 21:24–25 NIV).

So Jesus tells us to watch for unprecedented and terrifying events among the planets and stars, events which will affect our atmosphere and weather and our seas. Some of the predictions in the Apocalypse echo Jesus's warnings.

Already we are seeing some of the strange conditions in the skies Jesus forecast. One such phenomenon is the unidentified flying object—the UFO.

UFO

Authorities now admit that there have been confirmed sightings of unidentified flying objects. There are even some baffling cases where people under hypnosis say they were taken aboard UFOs by beings from space.

Reports held in U.S. Air Force files reveal that whatever these flying objects are, they move and turn at speeds unmatched by human technology.

It's my opinion that UFOs are real and that there will be a proven "close encounter of the third kind" soon. And I believe that the source of this phenomenon is some type of alien being of great intelligence and power.

According to the Bible, a demon is a spiritual personality in a state of war with God. Prophecy tells us that demons will be allowed to use their powers of deception in a grand way during the last days of history (Thessalonians 2:8-12). I believe these demons will stage a spacecraft landing on Earth. They will claim to be from an advanced culture in another galaxy.

They may even claim to have "planted" human life on this planet and tell us they have returned to check on our progress. Many scientists—not to mention movies and television shows—are putting forth similar theories about the origin of life on Earth.

If demons led by Satan, their chief, did pull off such a deception, then they could certainly lead the world into total error regarding God and His revelation. They could even give a false explanation for the sudden disappearance of all the world's Christians—which will happen in the final days. But more about that later.

FOUR
UP AGAINST THE WALL

"Everywhere you turn in Israel today the Bible is coming to life. I'm not talking only about archeological discoveries, but about the international political scene as it affects us today. If you read the Biblical prophecies about Armageddon and the end days, and you look at the current realities in the world and especially the Middle East, things certainly begin to look familiar.

"The vast number of archeological discoveries in Israel have all tended to vindicate the pictures that are presented in the Bible. If therefore the Bible has been proven true concerning the past, we cannot look lightly at any prognostication it makes about the future."

—Major General Chaim Herzog,
Israeli ambassador to the United
Nations (from a 1977 interview
for the film *"The Late Great
Planet Earth"*)

In 1976, while doing research for a film in Israel, I had the pleasure of talking with one of that country's most brilliant and aggressive generals. We discussed the Yom Kippur War of 1973. Specifically, I wanted to find out about the disturbing changes I had noticed in Israel's economy, morale and general spirit of confidence since that war was fought.

THE MASADA CONNECTION

During our discussion, I brought up the "Masada Complex." This term is based on the heroics of the last of the Jews to stand against Titus and the Roman legions after the invaders had taken Jerusalem in 70 A.D.

For three years after Jerusalem fell, 950 brave men, women and children fought off the mighty Roman army from a plateau fortress built by King Herod near the Dead Sea. Finally, Titus used Jewish slaves to build an earthen ramp to the top of the fortress walls.

As the enraged Romans were about to breach the walls, the Jews inside voted to take a desperate action. Rather than see their children tortured, their wives raped and all survivors condemned to slavery, they voted unanimously to take their own lives. When Titus and his soldiers stormed the fort, they won a hollow victory.

In modern Israel, all military officers are sworn in with an emotional ceremony at Masada, which still stands. Part of their oath states, "Masada shall never fall again."

This willingness to fight to the death rather than have the nation of Israel destroyed and its people scattered again became labeled "the Masada Complex." The term was used frequently to describe Israel's fighting spirit during the '50s and '60s.

THE SAMSON COMPLEX

I asked the general if the Israelis still had the "Masada Complex." You can imagine how startled I was when he quickly replied, "We no longer have the Masada Complex. We now have the Samson Complex."

The general knew that I was familiar with the Bible, and he watched for my reaction with a mix of curiosity and slight humor.

It didn't take me long to grasp the awesome significance of the new attitude. Immediately I saw how it explained what had happened in Israel since the Yom Kippur War of 1973.

You see, at Masada the Israelis took their own lives rather than be conquered. But when Samson chose death over slavery, he destroyed his enemies as well. It doesn't take a vivid imagination to see how this applies to the current Middle East situation.

WHEN ISRAEL ALMOST FELL

A hint of Israel's new outlook was revealed just after the 1973 war. *Time* magazine quoted a conversation between General Moshe Dayan, then chief of Israel's defense, and the late Prime Minister Golda Meir. The conversation reportedly took place when Israel's defenses were being overwhelmed both in the Sinai and in the Golan Heights.

"The Third Temple (a term for modern Israel) is falling," Dayan reportedly told his prime minister. "Arm the dooms-day weapon."

One of the world's worst-kept military secrets is that Israel has strategic nuclear capabilities. Few military experts doubt that the Israelis could prepare to launch a nuclear attack in just a few days time.

NEVER AGAIN

Anyone who understands the history of the Jewish people knows what the Israelis would do if they found themselves about to fall to their Arab enemies. Drastic action seems called for when you see the vicious propaganda which so vividly portrays the slaughter of the Jews.

Consider the history of the Jews. They have wandered from one country to another since Rome destroyed their nation in 70 A.D. History is littered with one persecution of the Jews after another—the Inquisitions, the pogroms of Russia, Hitler's death camps, to name just a few. But through it all, the Jews have remained a distinct race.

Knowing all that, I'm sure that if Israel saw its own destruction near it would use whatever was needed to bomb key Arab cities right off the map.

In fact, I wouldn't be surprised if Israel launched an attack on Russia as well, since the Soviets have armed and goaded Israel's Arab enemies. Remember, Israel has the capability of producing nuclear weapons, and its pilots are legends for their skill and daring.

If the world were to stand by and allow another holocaust to occur, then, like Samson of old, Israel would surely take its enemies along to mutual destruction.

THE GRIM CHANGE

This is the bleak situation that has developed in the 10 years since I wrote *The Late Great Planet Earth*. It's time now to trace the key events of the past decade to show how Israel has arrived at its current perilous position.

Once the past is understood I will show how the stage is being set for the final events which will lead to the coming of the Messiah.

In 1970, Israel was confident. The Israelis still savored the brilliant victory of the June 1967 war. Israel was respected, even if not loved, by most of the world's nations. A steady flow of immigrants, so vital to the country's survival, rushed to Israel's shores.

The Israeli economy, too, seemed to be thriving, and the outlook was bright. The average citizen enjoyed a letup of the dual pressures to support a family and defend the nation.

And the outlook for peace was bright. After all, the Israelis reasoned, it looked as though it would take at least 10 years for the Arab losers of the Six Day War to recover and retrain and rearm their troops.

THE HOMECOMING

The Israelis were euphoric over possessing at last Old Jerusalem, the very soul of the Jew. During 2,000 years of dispersion throughout the world, the wandering Jew wrote longing songs, poems and prose about his return to Jerusalem. Now it had happened.

Even the non-religious Jew feels a mystical tug when he visits the last remnant of the ancient temple, now known as the "wailing wall" (the site is the retaining wall on the west side of a temple built by Solomon and refurbished by Herod in the time of Jesus).

The wall is the symbol of the unity of the Jews as a race and of their ancient ties to God. Even battle-hardened soldiers wept when they first approached the wall. I have stood by many a Jew when he first touched the wall, and all have felt that at last they had come home. So did I.

General Moshe Dayan expressed the feeling of all Israelis in 1967, when he stood with his weeping soldiers at the wall and proclaimed, "We have returned to our holiest of holy places, never to leave her again."

Remember well all I have said here about the intensity of Jewish feeling toward Jerusalem. It will be crucial if we are to understand the events which have been predicted, and, I believe, will occur in the 1980's. But I'm rushing ahead; let's look at the changes in Israel since the beginning of the '70s.

THE YOM KIPPUR WAR

In 1973, Israel's brief period of optimism was dashed. On the Day of Atonement, the holiest day of the Jewish calendar, Israeli forces were caught off guard.

Attackers from Syria hit the Golan Heights with hundreds of the finest Russian-made tanks. The vastly-outnumbered Israeli tank forces were hit even harder by newly-designed Soviet anti-tank weapons. These new arms almost won the war before Israel had a chance to fight back.

I discussed the fighting with one of the few Israeli tank commanders in the Golan Heights who survived the first day of battle. He told me that by afternoon only a few Israeli tanks stood between 1,200 Syrian tanks and the city of Tiberias, in the north. The Syrian forces were poised to over-run that region.

Providentially, the Syrian commander falsely suspected a trap because the gains were made too easily. He ordered a stop for lunch to figure out the situation.

It was during that two-hour lunch break that Israeli reinforcements arrived and turned back the Syrians. But it was a costly victory.

THE SOUTHERN FRONT

To the south, Egyptian forces had won a similar early victory. Under the umbrella of new Russian-made antiaircraft missiles, the Egyptians broke through Israel's first line of defense and destroyed many Israeli tanks.

Numerous Israeli planes and pilots were lost on both the northern and the southern fronts. New Russian-made ground-to-air missiles had seen to that.

If God had not been with Israel during this war, I don't believe that nation would exist today. By the war's end, the Israelis secured an even greater victory than they had in 1967. But the victory came at a great cost.

ISRAEL WEEPS AGAIN

There was hardly a family in Israel which had not lost a relative in the fighting. In such a small country, the grief is multiplied. The equipment loss, too, was appalling. Add the replacement costs to Israel's huge defense debt and the burden is staggering.

The cost of replacing military equipment is one of the major reasons for Israel's current economic woes. The Israeli pays the highest taxes in the world. The inflation rate is nearly 100 percent a year. The average Israeli man must hold two jobs to support his family. And those men have to serve in the military for at least one month a year.

EXODUS OF THE '70S

After the Yom Kippur War, the immigration of foreign citizens which Israel depended so heavily upon began to fall. In fact, many Israelis started emigrating to other nations.

Also, constant terrorist attacks against Israelis at home and abroad caused the nation more grief. The Munich Olympics massacre, the Ma'alot attack and the Entebbe plane hijacking are but a few such incidents.

INTERNATIONAL PERILS

Besides its troubles at home, Israel faces new perils from around the world. During the 1970's, many critical international changes took place.

The OPEC Peril

First, there is the Organization of Petroleum Exporting Countries.

During the 1973 war, the Arab nations finally learned to use their oil as a powerful weapon. They found that they could use their precious product to force nations to turn against Israel.

The pressure worked. A squadron of giant U.S. C-5 transport planes carrying badly-needed equipment from America to Israel almost didn't make it.

No European country would allow the planes to land and refuel for fear of angering the Arabs. Finally, Portugal let the planes land at the Azores Island air base. But there is no guarantee that Portugal will be so friendly next time, as that nation's government has since changed.

The Iranian Peril

The second danger comes from the chaos in Iran. Israel used to buy a large portion of its oil from the Iranians because their leader, the shah, was pro-Israel.

But when the Ayatollah Khomeini stepped into power, the flow of oil stopped. The ayatollah's first official audience after he seized power was with Yasser Arafat, leader of the rabidly anti-Israel Palestine Liberation Organization (the P.L.O.)

Now Israel must depend on the U.S. for emergency oil supplies, especially since the Israelis returned the Sinai oil fields to Egypt. There's only one problem: Where will *we* get the oil?

The Islamic Peril

At the start of the 1970's, Israel only had Russia and 130 million enemy Arabs to worry about. But with the "Islamic Revival" sparked by the Ayatollah Khomeini, all the world's Moslems have lined up against Israel. This includes much of black Africa as well as the Moslem population which extends from Pakistan into the Pacific region.

The False Peace Peril

Many people attached great hope to the recent Egypt-Israel peace accord. Certainly, Egypt's president Anwar Sadat did a brave thing when he initiated direct negotiations with Israel. But I doubt that Sadat will be able to keep the nations moving toward peace.

One reason I feel that way is that Sadat is in constant danger of being assassinated by militant Arabs. Several attempts to kill him have already been reported. If he were to die, it is fairly certain that someone more radical would replace him.

Also, I doubt that Israeli Prime Minister Menachem Begin will be either willing or able to turn over enough land concessions to satisfy Sadat. The Arabs expect the peace initiative to regain the Gaza Strip, the West Bank and East Jerusalem.

And it's clear to anyone who knows the situation that the Israelis will probably never allow the establishment of an autonomous Palestinian state on the West Bank.

It's just as clear that under no circumstances will Israel return Old Jerusalem to the Arabs. Remember what I reported earlier about the Jewish passion for the city of Jerusalem.

Now suppose that Egypt once again became an enemy of Israel. It could easily happen. Egyptians and other Arabs could place such pressure on Sadat for his failure to regain Palestinian rights that he would have to give in to their demands or be removed from office.

In such a case, Israel would be in desperate peril. The Sinai buffer zone is already gone. So is most of the oil supply. And Egypt, which has many of the U.S.'s top-of-the-line F-16 fighter planes, would be a dangerous enemy.

The Ally Peril

Outside the Middle East, Israel's position isn't much better. Except for the U.S., Israel has no allies.

France was once something of an ally. Israel bought most of its aircraft from the French during the '50s and '60s. But France is hungry for Arab oil. Today, Israel cannot even buy replacement parts for its French-built Mirage fighter planes.

We are still Israel's friend. But there are strong pressures from within to turn away from Israel. I pray that we do not, for our friendship with the Israelis is one of the reasons we've survived as a nation. But I'll say more about that later.

THE ODDS AGAINST ISRAEL

So this is Israel's grim situation today, surrounded by millions of fanatical enemies. The Arabs have turned almost the entire Third World against the Israelis. All Moslems see Israel as their enemy. And Russia and its satellites are right behind those foes. Every other nation except for the U.S. refuses to side with Israel for fear of losing Arab oil.

But don't count Israel out yet. The God of Israel has sworn in the prophecies that He will not forsake the Israelis, nor let them be destroyed.

CURRENT WISDOM FROM
OLD PROPHETS

The prophets are very clear about the facts we must consider at this point in history.

First, they told us, once Israel is reborn as a nation, in the last days, it will never be destroyed or removed from the land again (Ezekiel 36:22–36; 38:8–16 and 39:23–29). So whatever perils Israel now faces will not destroy that nation.

Second, these prophets forecast that Israel will be brought to the brink of annihilation just before the coming of the Messiah, who will save the Israelis (see Zachariah chapters 12–14 and especially chapter 13, verses eight and nine). According to Ezekiel, Israel's great crisis will cause many Jews to believe in their true Messiah.

Zachariah speaks of this holocaust and the repentence which follows: "And I will pour out on the House of David and all the inhabitants of Jerusalem the spirit of grace and supplication, so that they will look on Me whom they have pierced; and they will mourn for Him as one mourns for an only son" (Zachariah 12:10).

As God speaks in the above verse, He raises the most incredible question. Remember, this was written 500 years before Christ.

The question is this: When did Israel "pierce" God? If you are a Jew reading this and the meaning is still unclear, I challenge you to turn to Isaiah chapter 53 right now. You will find your answer.

Finally, the prophets told us that a great northern confederacy will launch an all-out attack on the Middle East and Israel in particular (Ezekiel 38 and Daniel 11:40–45). For two centuries, Christian and Jewish scholars have identified this northern power as being Russia. (For more details see *The Late Great Planet Earth*.)

This Soviet invasion is certainly forseeable now. Russia's attack on Afghanistan was its first step into the pages of Ezekiel, chapter 38. It's clear that the Russian strategy is to cut off the supply of Persian Gulf oil to the west and then close all sea lanes leading to that vital area (more on this in a later chapter).

For Russia to secure this region, it must attempt to destroy Israel, the one viable military power in the Middle East which could resist Soviet troops.

PROFILE OF THE FALSE PROPHET

Before any of the prophecies just mentioned can be fulfilled, there must be a period of great danger and desperation in Israel.

I believe the prophetic significance of Israel's present situation, described in this chapter, will set the stage for an even greater danger. I say even greater because it will decide the destiny of men's souls, not the mere disposition of their mortal lives.

According to the prophets, a Jewish false prophet will arise in Israel at the height of its turmoil. He is described in Revelation (13:11–17) as a miracle-working man who will masquerade as the Jewish messiah.

He will lead Israel to worship the leader of the great 10-nation European confederacy. This leader, who will appear to be good, is known in prophecy as "the anti-Christ."

THE COVENANT OF DEATH

The Jewish false prophet will lead Israel to sign a covenant of protection with the anti-Christ, a treaty Isaiah described as a "covenant with death" and a "pact with hell" (Isaiah 28:14–18).

In exchange for the European leader's protection and a guarantee of temple rights in Old Jerusalem, Israel will sign the treaty and worship the Jewish false prophet as the messiah and the anti-Christ as God Himself (Daniel 9:27 and 2 Thessalonians 2:3–11).

Is Israel at this point today? My blood ran cold a few years ago when I heard an Israeli say, "I would worship the Devil if he would bring peace and security to the Middle East." I believe the false prophet is in the Middle East today, awaiting his fateful hour.

THE MESSIAH MAKES U.P.I.

On Jan. 6, 1980, I was electrified as I listened to the news on my car radio. A United Press International correspondent, Howard Arenstein, reported from Jerusalem that three aged Rabbis had each independently recounted dreams that the Messiah was coming soon. The reporter said all of Israel was excitedly talking about the dreams.

In a follow-up newspaper article by Arenstein, many amazing statements were made by various Rabbis.

Arenstein wrote: "Bible scholars said many signs do exist that the Messiah may arrive soon. Followers of Menachem Schneerson, a Brooklyn Rabbi, said their leader sees imminent danger for Israel in the tense Middle East situation and issued special orders for prayer and fasting. 'The general situation in the world is such that only the Messiah can save it,' a spokesman for the Rabbi said."

Arenstein continued: "The chief Rabbi of Jerusalem, Moroccan-born Shlomo Masbah, dismissed the dreams, but he said he does believe the Messiah may be on His way.

"Shabetai Shiloh, who is said to have forecast the October Arab-Israel war, said the Messiah will come soon. Shiloh said the war marked the first of three rounds of fighting heralding the Messiah's arrival.

"In the second round, all the nations of the world must be angry with Israel, Shiloh said. He thinks the destruction of an Arab capital by Israeli forces would create that situation.

"The third round, Shiloh said, will be a three month war between the superpowers. He quoted a religious leader of the last century, the Gaon of Wilnah, who said, 'When the Russians enter Turkey, then we must prepare festive clothes to greet the Messiah.'

" 'Today, that's a real possibility,' Shiloh said."[1]

NO NEUTRALS

Doesn't all this sound familiar? Obviously the Rabbis have been studying Ezekiel chapter 38.

I believe all this evidence can mean only one thing: The situation in Israel is becoming so desperate that the Jews are now ready for a messiah. But the messiah who comes will be that arch deceiver, the false prophet.

Because the Rabbis have worked so hard to reject Jesus of Nazareth as the messiah, the whole area of messianic prophecy has been obscured and not truly investigated. Without an honest and open-minded evaluation of passages like Isaiah 53, Isaiah 49:5–7 and Isaiah 35:5–7 (to name just a few) we have no standard to judge one claiming to be a messiah true or false.

The time is at hand when men will either find the true Messiah or they will be deceived into believing in a false messiah. There will be no neutrals.

Where will you stand?

FIVE
THE CRESCENT
OF CRISIS

"They have said, 'Come, and let us wipe them out as a nation; That the name of Israel be remembered no more.' "

—Psalm 83:4

In the Bible, the reborn state of Israel is predicted as the center of the events that will lead to the last war of the world. Israel is literally the fuse of Armageddon—a prophetic name for the last war.

And the Arabs are portrayed as the spark that will light the fuse. Because of the 4,000 year-old animosity between these two ancient races, the Hebrew Prophets say they will fight a battle into which all of the world's nations will be drawn.

I first read these predictions in 1955. When I saw that the pattern of future world events would center around the Middle East, I was amazed.

How could a conflict between the rather backward and underdeveloped Arab countries and the tiny state of Israel become so important to the great powers of the world? I asked myself, who wants all that sand? Sure, there was oil. But 25 years ago that just didn't seem to be enough to draw the world's superpowers into an all-out war.

Yet that was exactly what was predicted, and it is exactly what is happening.

By 1973, 13 years after the oil cartel was formed, what *should* have been obvious became too clear to miss: The Middle East, because of its oil reserves, would soon be the most stragetic area in the world.

THE ARABS RISE TO POWER

How did the Arabs go from weakness and disarray in the early 1970's, just 10 years ago, to their current state of power? Let's take a look. In 1970:

• They were still despondent over their crushing defeat at the hands of the Israelis in 1967.

• They lacked a basic unifying force strong enough to overcome their fierce independence and the rivalries which existed between their nations and tribes for centuries.

• Powerful, oil-rich Iran was still an ally to the U.S., the rest of the west and Israel.

EXPLOSIVE IN THE '80S

As the '80s begin, the Arabs have shed their second-class status. I'll list the conditions which have changed so you can see how the stage is being set for the fulfillment of the predictions. The events which are about to occur will lead us to the last great war. The speed at which these changes are fitting into the prophetic picture is a clear sign to students of prophecy.

Oil–The Achilles Heel

The Achilles Heel of the industrial nations is their need for oil. Entire economies stand or fall with the availability of petroleum. It influences every part of life in a modern industrial nation. From factories to transportation to farming to making synthetic fabrics to generating electricity, oil is the life-blood of the developed world.

The Organization of Petroleum Exporting Countries—

OPEC—has had the potential to influence the world since the time it was formed, in 1960.

But it wasn't until 1973 that the Arab oil barons showed the world how easily they could cut off the supply of petroleum. When they flexed that muscle, the world panicked.

Then OPEC brought western Europe, the U.S. and Japan to their knees by increasing the price of crude oil fourfold. This move staggered the economies of the industrial nations. It helped cause a very serious recession-inflation syndrome in the U.S., a condition which still exists.

The 1970's were marked by one economic spasm after another ripping through the western nations—mostly due to oil price hikes.

As the Arabs see it, it's only a matter of time before Israel's one true ally, the U.S., will become so dependent on Middle East oil that we will have to either drop our support of Israel or be destroyed economically.

This tactic has already worked on other nations, especially in western Europe. No nation there will show support for Israel for fear of losing a favored bargaining position for Arab oil.

The Cash Crisis

Another reason attention is focused on the Middle East is the enormous buildup of western currency there. As the price of oil rises, the wealth of the west flows in a growing flood to the Middle East oil exporters.

Never in history has there been such a rapid transfer of assets from one of the world's spheres of power to another. If they wish, the oil barons will soon be able to buy up the majority of the west's vital holdings.

To illustrate this threat, noted economist Ernest Conine said in 1974: "Within 10 years, according to a confidential study by the World Bank, this band of small countries could have more than $1 trillion on hand—more than enough to buy all the shares outstanding on the New York Stock Exchange."[1]

Members of OPEC have already brought major shares of some of the largest companies in Europe. They also own banks, farmland, real estate and businesses in the U.S. as well.

The fact is that as more and more money goes to these foreign countries, and as the western nations' balance of payments become more lopsided, then the Arabs will become even more powerful in determining the foreign policies of the world's major powers.

So if something bothers the Arabs, they now have two mighty tools—oil and money—to bring their grievances to the world's attention. And what grieves the Arabs? Israel, and particularly Jerusalem.

The Yom Kippur War

From the Arab point of view, this conflict changed the entire atmosphere in the Middle East. It proved that the Arabs could plan and launch a successful attack and inflict some defeats on the Israeli army. Strange as it may sound, this war, which the Arabs lost, saved face for them. It proved that Israel was not truly invincible, for the Israelis came close to losing that war in the early stages.

Egypt's Peace Initiative

Some people think Sadat's bold quest for peace with Israel is really going to succeed. I don't want to minimize the courageous efforts of both Sadat and Begin in this venture. But let's not be naive to the situation which has resulted from the peace talks.

Since the fragile accord between Israel and Egypt was signed, the other Arab nations have become even more determined to cast Israel out of Palestine. Most Arab countries have ceased trading with Egypt.

These nations have bitterly condemned Sadat as a traitor to the Arab cause. Some Arab states have even broken off diplomatic relations with Egypt. The Palestine Liberation Organization has vowed that it will never allow a truce with Israel to stand, no matter what must be done to break it.

Fears were immediately raised in the U.S. when President Sadat gave asylum to Iran's deposed shah. That decision widened the gap between Sadat and the rest of the Islamic world and put his life in even greater danger than it had already been.

Reportedly, the Ayatollah Khomeini has put out what is in effect an "Islamic contract" on Sadat. The Ayatollah has called on all faithful Moslems to try and kill the Egyptian leader. Khomeini has promised "special blessings of Allah" for the person who executes Anwar Sadat.

With all these tensions, however, a truce of sorts must be established sooner or later. Bible prophecy says a three year, six month "pseudo-peace" will be achieved by the efforts of the false prophet of Israel and the anti-Christ, the leader of the revived Roman empire.

But the false peace will be shattered by an attack on Israel by combined Arab forces (see *The Late Great Planet Earth* for details).

This full-fledged war between Israel and the Arabs will give the Soviets and their satellites the excuse to launch their long-awaited invasion of the Middle East.

The rest of the world's nations will be drawn into that war. And here comes Armageddon, a battle so horrible that only the Messiah's return can prevent the destruction of the planet Earth. Thank God, He will come. But the Bible says there will be "war and rumor of war" until He returns.

The Iranian Revolution

In 1979, perilous changes took place in the world's most critical area, the Persian Gulf. Shah Mohammed Reza Pahlavi was overthrown and the Ayatollah Khomeini harnessed a revolution. Israel and the U.S. lost a valuable ally in the Shah's Iran.

Iran (referred to in the Bible as Persia) was the bulwark of defense in the gulf area. Under the Shah, a credible force equipped with the most modern U.S.-made weapons was the only viable deterrent to a Soviet invasion of the Persian Gulf area.

Newsweek reported that, "Throughout the Nixon-Kissinger years, Washington relied on the Shah of Iran to keep the peace east of the Suez. With the Shah's fall a year ago, that policy was suddenly in shambles."[2]

Iran has been in chaos ever since. It's once-formidable armed forces are in disarray, with lack of discipline and uncertain leadership. Many of the army's highest-ranked and best trained officers have been executed by the Ayatollah's "Revolutionary Court." The once vaunted Iranian armed forces stood at 415,000 men. Military experts now say that 60 percent have deserted.[3] Much of Iran's once-powerful weaponry and military equipment sits idle for lack of maintenance and repair.

The Ayatollah's efforts to rule a modern country by an archaic Moslem form of theocracy has caused chaos in government as well. None of the Ayatollahs have experience at governing a country and they overrule the decisions of those who do have the experience. Most expert observers believe that today's Iran is a sitting duck for a communist takeover.

Khomeini's hand in heightening the Middle East crisis is not limited to weakening Iran in the eyes of the Soviets. He has enjoyed his greatest success by igniting an "Islamic revival" among the Shi'ite Moslems. He has called for Saudi Arabian members of his sect to rise up and overthrow members of a rival sect, the Wahhabis.

This danger was reported by *Newsweek* magazine in 1980: "The Shi'ites are Saudi citizens, and tensions between them and the ruling Wahhabis have been a part of the Saudi landscape for decades. But these have been heightened by the revolution in Iran and by radio broadcasts from across the Persian Gulf urging the Saudi Shi'ites to rise against their 'oppressors'."[4]

This is critical. A senior Western diplomat recently said, "Events in Iran and Afghanistan have left Saudi Arabia as the principal pillar of Western security in the Arab world."[5] If the ruling house of Saud were toppled, there would be no stability left in the Persian Gulf. The door would be open for the Russian conquest of the region.

In truth, it seems that door is already ajar. Many observers believe that the "students" who invaded the U.S. embassy in Iran were Marxist trained and inspired. Also, military experts believe the United States' inability to act quickly and decisively in the Iranian embassy takeover seemed to have encouraged the Russian invasion of Afghanistan.

THE ISLAMIC REVIVAL

I cannot overemphasize how important the recent world Islamic revival has been in whipping up a widespread anti-Israeli and anti-west front.

Now there is much more than a mutual hatred of Israel to unify the Arabs. There is a religious fervor that a charismatic Moslem leader could spark into a full-fledged "Jahid" or holy war.

When PLO chief Yasser Arafat spoke recently about the united Moslem condemnation of Russia's invasion of Afghanistan, he made an extremely important comment. "Now the U.S. wants to use this occasion to rally the Moslem world against the Soviet Union," he accused. "But the Moslem world is most concerned about Palestine and Jerusalem, and you must remember that."[6]

We must remember that well. It is a matter of Arab racial pride to regain Palestine for the Arab Palestinians. But it's a matter of sacred Islamic honor to once again control Jerusalem, Islam's third-holiest site. So the Islamic revival has turned Palestine and Jerusalem—indeed, the entire Middle East—into a flaming issue throughout the world of Islam.

That revival has also fulfilled a Biblical prophecy found in Ezekiel 38, a prophecy I noted in *The Late Great Planet Earth*. I interpreted the passage as meaning that many black African

countries would join the Arabs in their hatred of Israel. The
Moslem countries of Africa have done just that in the name of
Islamic unity.

I also said to watch for a Russian takeover of Iran. Ezekiel
38:5 predicts that the Persians will fight beside Russian
troops when they invade Israel. When I wrote this, in 1969,
Iran was not considered part of the Arab union. The Iranians
were strongly pro-west, they provided Israel with oil and
other support and they enjoyed a stable government. But the
Bible's prophets unerringly forecasted the current situation.

THE MECCA INVASION

A fanatical group of Moslems, followers of a self-
proclaimed Mahdi, or messiah-like liberator, brought even
more danger to the Middle East recently.

These armed zealots seized the Sacred Mosque in Mecca,
Saudi Arabia. They demanded that their leader, Mohammed
Al-Quraishi, be recognized as the long-awaited Islamic messiah who would lead all Moslems to victory over their
enemies.

These terrorists claimed to have been inspired to act by the
Iranian revolt. They said that Khomeini had brought a new
dawn to the Moslem world.

The uprising was eventually crushed, and many of the
invaders were executed. But not before a battle in which they
fought a brilliant defense and demonstrated signs of superior
military training.

Time magazine reported on the incident: "Documents
found on the bodies of several of the invaders established
that they were South Yemenis; some of their wallets contained pictures of Iran's Ayatollah Khomeini. It was clear that
they were well trained, probably in South Yemen by Russian
military advisors, and that the operation had been well
planned.

"Said one Western intelligence official in the Middle East:

'This was a direct attack against the House of Saud. You can be sure that the end of the battle of the Sacred Mosque is not the last we will hear of trouble in Saudia Arabia.' "[7]

So we can see the danger facing Saudi Arabia, a moderating voice in the Arab world and the biggest single supplier of oil to the United States.

THE SOUTH YEMEN CONNECTION

There is a clear and apparent danger developing in the middle of the "Crescent of Crisis" in South Yemen. That area has become the staging ground for Russian-led communists to spread revolution throughout the vital areas that control the entrance to the Persian Gulf and to the Red Sea-Suez Canal access.

Newsweek reported: "Saudi Arabia is deeply fearful of Marxist South Yemen, whose Soviet-equipped army is reputedly the best in the area.

"Recently, the Saudis charged that 'dozens' of Soviet generals and 'hundreds' of Cuban soldiers had been airlifted to South Yemen. 'The threat is clearly there,' says a Western diplomat. 'South Yemen could make mincement out of most Arab armies, including the Saudis.' "[8]

These are truly ominous reports from this critical area. The situation is incendiary, and it could erupt into the long-predicted battle of Armageddon right now, except for a few more events that must occur first.

THE ISLAMIC BOMB

The situation in the Middle East is terrible enough as it is. But recent reports of another development *make my blood run cold*. I read the following in *Time* magazine early in 1980: "Washington was alarmed by Pakistan's plan to build a uranium enrichment plant reportedly financed by Libya. In trying to dissuade Pakistan from creating an 'Islamic Bomb,' Washington has used both carrot and stick with equal lack of success."[9]

When I connected that report with a bit of news I heard not long ago, I was awed.

It seems while studying nuclear technology in the West, a brilliant young Pakistani student scientist, unwittingly aided by his professors, gained access to key information vital to the construction of nuclear weapons. When his motives were discovered, he suddenly disappeared. Later, mysteriously, he turned up—back in Pakistan.

Libya is reportedly backing the Pakistani A-bomb venture, which makes it doubly frightening. The Libyans have long supplied the PLO with money and weapons. Considering the fiery and militant nature of Libya's dictator, Colonel Qaddafi, it may not be long before even Palestinian terrorists have nuclear capabilities.

If—or when—that occurs, then the entire U.S. will face nuclear blackmail, for the PLO has blamed our country for Israel's continuing existence in Palestine.

Another radical Arab state, Iraq, has reportedly acquired the means to make nuclear weapons. Iraq has guaranteed oil to France and Italy if those countries will build a nuclear power plant and a uranium enrichment plant and provide nuclear fuel to the Iraqis.

According to recent news reports, Iraq is considering a merger with Syria. If this happens, and it's very probable, then three of the bitterest anti-West and anti-Israel countries in all the Arab world—Libya and Iraq-Syria—will have nuclear potential.

Israel's policy toward terrorism in the past has always been "an eye for an eye" or, more accurately, "an attack for an attack." So it is likely that if an Arab state would drop a nuclear bomb on Israeli land, Israel would send one right back. So suddenly—nuclear war is being waged in the Middle East. Then it will be "a city for a city."

A SUMMARY OF CRISES

The perils facing the Middle East fall into three categories.

The Power Of Oil

The oil-rich Arabs have learned to use their oil as a political weapon. As the U.S. and the rest of the industrialized world continues to depend on Mideast oil, the Arabs will gain more power to control the world situation. If nations don't give in to their pressure, the Arabs have the power to bankrupt them.

The Power of Islam

The recent Islam revival throughout the Middle East and Africa has bound the Moslem nations into a united, anti-West, anti-Israel front. These fanatical Moslems appear certain to gain the potential to launch nuclear terrorist attacks in the near future.

The Power Of Russia

The Russian invasion of Afghanistan has telegraphed the Soviet intention to take over the entire Middle East. Russian troops are already present in South Yemen and Ethiopia, and the fall of the Shah in nearby Iran has opened the door for a Soviet conquest of the strategic Persian Gulf area. The rest of the Middle East—including Saudi Arabia, which sits on one-quarter of the world's known oil reserves—appears to be an easy target for a Soviet takeover.

This area has now fit precisely into the pattern predicted for it. All that remains is for the Russians to make their predicted move.

SIX
THE BEAR MOVES SOUTHWARD

"When you see the Russian army begin to move southward and enter Turkey, put on your Sabbath garments and get ready to welcome the Messiah."

—Rabbi Chaim Valoshiner,
mid-19th century

"And you (Russia) will come from your place out of the remote parts of the north, you and many peoples with you . . . a great assembly and a mighty army. And you will come up against My people Israel like a cloud to cover the land. It will come about in the last days that I shall bring you against My land. . . ."

—the prophet Ezekiel
(38:15-16), 7th century B.C.

One of this generation's most obvious prophetic signs of the coming of the Messiah is the rise of Russia to world power.

For several centuries, both Rabbis and Christian theologians have identified the great northern power named in Ezekiel as being the Soviet Union. Three times in Ezekiel chapters 38 and 39 it is forecast that Israel's great enemy will come from the "extreme" or "uttermost" north. Just take a globe and run your finger due north from Israel; you'll find yourself smack in the middle of Russia.

(I provided much documentation concerning Ezekiel's predictions for Russia in *The Late Great Planet Earth*. I also identified the nations which will fight alongside the Soviets.)

So according to Ezekiel, the "splendidly equipped" Russian army and its satellites will mount an all-out invasion of the Middle East.

THE BEAR AND IRAN

Before Russia attacks Israel, however, it will first invade Iran, or Persia, as it is called in Ezekiel chapter 38, verse five.

When we apply this prophecy to modern times, it becomes obvious that the Soviets will use their recent conquest of Afghanistan as a springboard to overthrow Iran and gain control of the Persian Gulf area.

Russia may decide to use a well-equipped satellite country such as Iraq to gain control of Iran. Although Iraq pulled away from the Soviets after the invasion of Afghanistan, don't be surprised if the differences are reconciled. It's also conceivable that Iran could fall from within to the evergrowing Iranian Marxists.

RUSSIA ASCENDS TO WORLD POWER

As recently as 20 years ago, it seemed unlikely that Russia would become the world's greatest military power. Today, the Soviets are without a question the strongest power on the face of the earth. Let's look at recent history to see how the Russians rose to the might predicted for them thousands of years ago.

In 1962, during the Cuban missile crisis, the Russians still had a grudging but healthy respect for the U.S. and the Western powers. That was because the U.S. still had a clear strategic weapons lead. But America let that lead—and the respect that went with it—slip away (see exhibit II).

Exhibits II and III show the incredible advantage the U.S. had over the U.S.S.R. in strategic weapons in 1964.

The United States had more than a four to one advantage in the number of ICBMs; a 10 to one advantage in SLBMs (submarine launched ballistic missiles) and a 17 to one advantage in total deliverable nuclear warheads. As you can see from exhibit III, the U.S. had 6,800 nuclear warheads compared to only 400 for the Soviets.

In addition, America's 1,300 strategic bomber planes gave it a better than seven to one edge over the U.S.S.R.'s 1970.

By 1980, the picture had changed radically. Today the Soviets have unbelievable advantages in the number of

ICBMs, the number of ICBM warheads, the number of SLBMs and in total deliverable megatonage. Currently, the U.S. leads in total number of warheads only because the U.S. has more short-range *low* yield sub-launched warheads.

The Russians have 70 percent more ICBMs than the U.S. has, and 58 percent more SLBMs. Most alarming, the Russians have a six to one lead in deliverable megatonage, an edge that will increase to 10 to one by 1983. In that year, Soviet warheads will be able to carry a total of 13,239 megatons of payload, compared to the 1,300 megaton payload U.S. missiles will carry (see exhibit IV).

Not only has the U.S. surrendered its once-enormous advantage in strategic missiles, but it has reduced its bomber force from 1,300 planes in 1964 to just 414 in 1980. All those bombers are sub-sonic and, because of their age and slowness, are considered obsolete by many experts. Meanwhile, the Russians have sharply increased bomber production to give them a total of 675, a 63 percent advantage.

HOW COULD THE U.S. GIVE UP ITS SUPERIORITY?

The United States was far ahead in the nuclear arms race until the end of the 1960's. Then the situation began to change rapidly. This change occurred because of the U.S. leadership's almost unbelievable misreading of the Soviet goals and intentions. In light of the clearly-stated communist goal of world domination and their constant efforts to attain that status, it is incomprehensible to me that America allowed the Russians to take the lead in the arms race.

To understand how the U.S. slipped into this perilous position we must review some recent history. This is not intended to be a lesson in political science but rather an illustration of how current events have taken the world to the point the Bible predicted for the last days.

EXHIBIT II

NUMBER OF ICBM'S AND MOBILE ICBM'S
1964

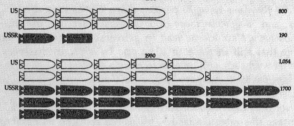

US   800

USSR   190

1980

US   1,054

USSR   1700

SUB-LAUNCHED BALLISTIC MISSILES
1964

US   300

USSR   29

1980

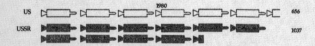

US   656

USSR   1037

STRATEGIC BOMBERS
1964

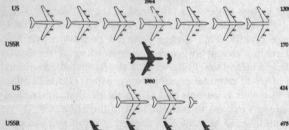

US   1300

USSR   170

1980

US   414

USSR   675

FIGURES COMPILED FROM DEPARTMENT OF DEFENSE AND THE COALITION FOR PEACE THROUGH STRENGTH.

EXHIBIT III
TOTAL NUCLEAR WARHEADS

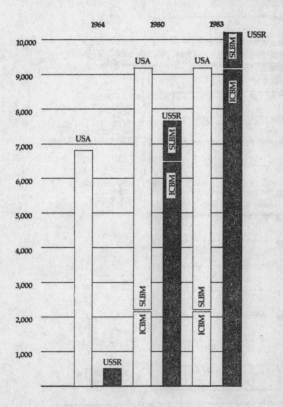

FIGURES COMPILED FROM DEPARTMENT OF DEFENSE AND THE COMMITTEE ON THE PRESENT DANGER.

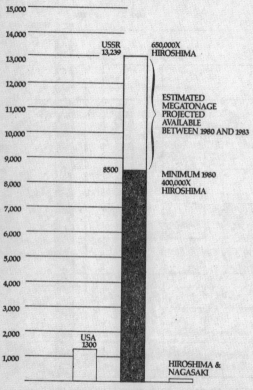

EXHIBIT IV
TOTAL DELIVERABLE MEGATONAGE—
1980-1983

FIGURES COMPILED FROM DEPARTMENT OF DEFENSE AND THE COALITION FOR PEACE THROUGH STRENGTH.

EXHIBIT V
DEFENSIVE WEAPONS—1980

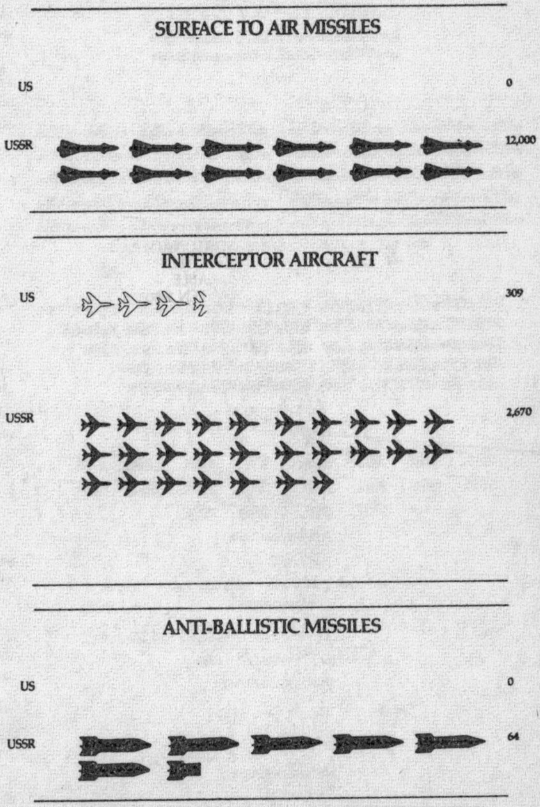

SURFACE TO AIR MISSILES

US   0

USSR   12,000

INTERCEPTOR AIRCRAFT

US   309

USSR   2,670

ANTI-BALLISTIC MISSILES

US   0

USSR   64

FIGURES COMPILED FROM DEPARTMENT OF DEFENSE AND THE COALITION FOR PEACE THROUGH STRENGTH.

EXHIBIT VI
CONVENTIONAL FORCES

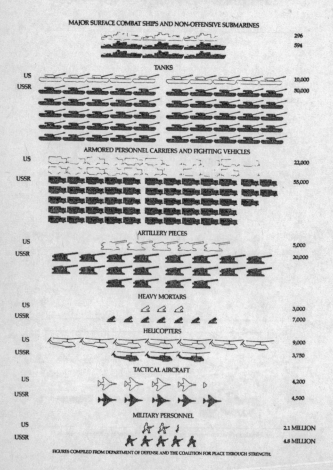

MAJOR SURFACE COMBAT SHIPS AND NON-OFFENSIVE SUBMARINES

296
594

TANKS

US — 10,000
USSR — 50,000

ARMORED PERSONNEL CARRIERS AND FIGHTING VEHICLES

US — 22,000
USSR — 55,000

ARTILLERY PIECES

US — 5,000
USSR — 20,000

HEAVY MORTARS

US — 3,000
USSR — 7,000

HELICOPTERS

US — 9,000
USSR — 3,750

TACTICAL AIRCRAFT

US — 4,200
USSR — 4,500

MILITARY PERSONNEL

US — 2.1 MILLION
USSR — 4.8 MILLION

FIGURES COMPILED FROM DEPARTMENT OF DEFENSE AND THE COALITION FOR PEACE THROUGH STRENGTH.

NAVAL CHIEF OF STAFF SPEAKS OUT

On July 17, 1979, Admiral Elmo R. Zumwalt, Jr., gave shocking testimony to the U.S. Senate Committee on Foreign Relations. Admiral Zumwalt was a member of the Joint Chiefs of Staff and was director of Arms Control for the Secretary of Defense in 1962 and 1963.

Zumwalt's testimony reveals the secret of how the Soviet Union was able to surpass the U.S. and become the mightiest military power on Earth, just as the prophets predicted. Here is an excerpt from his testimony:

> In the aftermath of the Cuban missile crisis, President Kennedy and Secretary (of Defense) NcNamara made the bold and idealistic decision to begin a dialogue with the Soviet Union designed to achieve a fair and balanced strategic nuclear relationship.
>
> Their speeches and policy statements to Congress and their discussions with Soviet officials sought to put a new theory across. The essence of the message was as follows:
>
> *"The U.S. recognizes that its strategic nuclear superiority is unacceptable to the Soviet Union. We understand that your attempt to install missiles in Cuba was an effort to redress that imbalance. We propose now to let you catch up to us. We shall then have a situation of mutual assured destruction or mutual deterrence.*
>
> *"We propose to stop at the 1,054 ICBMs and 656 SLBMs we are now building. You should do the same. We propose to keep our missiles with a combination of size and accuracy that you will know from your own calculations that we cannot destroy yours in a first strike, so that you could always retaliate if we struck first. You should do the same with regard to size and accuracy.*
>
> *"Both sides should reduce the continuing radiation produced by the warheads to minimize the kill of innocents if military targets should be struck. Each side should forego civil defense so that cities of each would be hostage against their own government's first strike."*

To show good faith, the U.S. gradually reduced its expenditures for strategic nuclear arms to one-third of the constant dollar budgets of the period 1956-1962 over the next decade and a half.

In retrospect, it is clear that the Soviet Union and the U.S. reacted exactly oppositely in their policies and programs after the Cuban missile crisis. In essence, our proposed dialogue remained a monologue.

The Soviets accelerated their strategic nuclear weapons expenditures, outspending us for many years, today by threefold. They proceeded to build asymmetrical advantages in each of the areas of suggested constraint.

In order to get them to sign the SALT I interim offensive agreement a decade later, we had to grant them nearly a 55 percent advantage in ICBMs—1,618 to our earlier proposed 1,054. They had the option to reduce to a 35 percent advantage in ICBMs in order to exercise their option to build up to a 35 percent advantage in SLBMs, which they have been doing.

At the signing of SALT I, because the Soviets had disregarded the suggested constraint on size, they had about a 300 percent advantage in megatonage and throw weight.

While we have greatly reduced the fallout produced by our warheads, they have maintained full fallout lethality so that their weapons will kill innocents for hundreds of square miles around targets they hit. And while we have truly foregone civil defense, the Soviets have made major expenditures to develop underground shelter, population evacuation and industrial survival procedures.

THE STRATEGIC SELLOUT

The U.S. deliberately slowed down in the arms race so that the U.S.S.R. could catch up and feel more secure and peaceful. The fatal assumption behind this thinking was that the Russians truly wanted peace, and that if America would just stop scaring them with all its nuclear missiles then they would gladly use restraint in acquiring their own strategic weapons.

The U.S.'s leaders let the Russians know of their willingness to slow down the arms race. Eagerly, the Soviets pushed for talks to draft a Strategic Arms Limitation Treaty (SALT) in 1963.

After the talks began the U.S.S.R. started outspending the U.S. by **three to one** in the development of nuclear weapons and delivery systems.

At the same time, the U.S. cut back on arms spending and intentionally stopped developing and deploying strategic weapons. America actually threw away its costly and hard won superiority. And, as history bears out, the U.S. lost its most effective deterrent to Soviet expansionism. We have also fallen radically behind in our defensive and conventional weapons, as graphically portrayed in Exhibits V and VI.

All these concessions were based on the assumption that the U.S. could trust the Russians, despite the fact that the U.S.S.R. had been a source of aggression in the world since the end of World War II.

CAN WE TRUST THE SOVIETS?

Sure we can trust them! But only in one area. We can trust the Russians to follow their communist doctrines and beliefs to the letter. But because of one of the fundamental doctrines of communist philosophy, we cannot trust them in any other way.

In the philosophy of Marxism-Leninism, there is no such thing as right or wrong, truth or lie apart from the effect on the state and its goals. Since the communists believe that there is no God, all truth is relative. The concept of an absolute truth that is always true does not exist in communist thinking. The state takes the place of God, and so it can redefine truth however and whenever a change is needed to reach a goal.

Something which is "true" becomes "untrue" when it ceases to serve the communist goal of world domination. To a communist, it would be a "sin" to continue abiding by a treaty that no longer benefits "God," the state.

Historically, U.S. thinking says it is immoral to break a solemn promise made in a treaty (although that moral sense is deteriorating as our country continues to move away from its founding faith in Biblical ethics). But to the communist mind, it is immoral to keep an agreement when it no longer serves the goal of "liberating the world for communism."

COMMUNISM IS A RELIGION

To understand the communist mind and its motivations, you must first realize that communism is more of a religion than a political philosophy. It is a religion based on certain erroneous concepts of man and his nature.

Communism believes that man has no soul. He secretes thoughts and a personality just as a stomach secretes digestive juices. Man is purely a material being whose nature can be shaped by his environment, the communists say. Change the environment and you change the man. This notion is diametrically opposed to Judeo-Christian thought.

Marxist-Leninists believe that they have discovered the fundamental laws which shape men and history. The number one corrupter of mankind, they say, is capitalism and the free enterprise system. Private ownership of property and a competitive economic system make men selfish, greedy and aggressive, the communists believe.

THE ELITE DICTATORSHIP

When the communists took over Russia in 1917, they established a "ruling elite" which viewed itself as the vanguard of the revolutionary society. Members of this elite claimed they were entrusted with the responsibility of changing "the very nature of man."

This elite believed that such a change cannot take place

until the working people of the world (those who do not own property) rise up against their property-owning masters (the capitalists) and overthrow them.

When all vestiges of capitalism in the world have been rooted out and destroyed, and the people own all things through the state, then the "power elite" will serve only as benevolent administrators of the common good.

THE SUPREME GOAL

When that happens—when capitalism has been wiped off the face of the earth—then the supreme goal of the communists can be reached. With no capitalism to "corrupt" him, man will become a peace-loving creature who lives only to work and share with his neighbor. And thus the supreme goal of communism—to change man's nature—will be achieved.

So the end result of communism cannot be realized until its disciples "liberate the people from the sinful capitalists who have corrupted mankind and caused misery and war." Communism, because of its very nature, must continue to overthrow and expand. The communists believe there can be no peace while capitalism still exists.

EXAMPLES OF "THE COMMUNIST MAN"

Josef Stalin, an architect of the Soviet system, made communism's goal clear: "As long as capitalism and socialism exist, we cannot live in peace. In the end one or the other will triumph—a funeral dirge will be sung either over the Soviet republic or over world capitalism."[1]

The late Soviet premier Nikita Khrushchev later echoed Stalin's view during a visit to the U.S. when he thundered, "We will bury you!"

I cannot resist raising a question here. If communism will

change man's nature for the good, why has it produced such bestiality in its leaders?

A case in point is Stalin. Even the Supreme Soviet Council of the U.S.S.R. has condemned him for his awful crimes against his own people. His name has even been removed from monuments in Russia. Many other leaders, such as Khrushchev, have also been denounced by fellow communists.

Six million Ukrainians were starved to death because they rejected communism. Millions more have been executed, tortured, imprisoned and exiled because their thoughts ran counter to the party line.

China's Mao Tse-tung was responsible for more murders than any other tyrant known to history. Even Hitler looks moderate next to Stalin and Mao.

COMMUNISM'S "NON-AGGRESSIVE" RECORD

So much for the "peace-loving" side of communism. How about its "non-aggressive" nature? According to a recent study, that claim is also false. In a report titled, "What is the Soviet Union Up To?" the Committee on the Present Danger, a Washington, D.C.-based group said: "No empire in history has expanded so aggressively as the Russian. The Soviet Union is the only great power to have emerged from World War II larger than it was in 1939."

Exhibit VII shows how Soviet-backed communism has spread throughout the world since the Russian revolution of 1917.

THE YALTA DISASTER

How was this incredible expansion allowed to happen? The western powers made a crucial mistake just after World

EXHIBIT VII
THE GROWTH OF COMMUNISM

Beginning with President Kennedy, each U.S. administration has grossly misjudged the goals of the Soviet Union and communism in general.

Each successive administration has hoped that its own example of fairness and good will toward the world would somehow encourage the communists to abandon their drive toward world domination.

We've proclaimed "detente" and pretended that the Soviets were no longer the "bad guys," but rather were just as interested in peace as we were.

The table that follows clearly demonstrates that the Soviets are just as dedicated to their ruthless plan of world domination today as they were in 1917. Since the 1930s, not a decade has passed without millions of people falling under the tyranny of communism.

Country	Year of Communist Takeover	Country	Year of Communist Takeover
Mongolia	1924	East Germany	1948
Bessarabia; Bukovina	1940	China	1949
Estonia	1940	North Vietnam	1954
Latvia	1940	Cuba	1960
Lithuania	1940	South Yemen	1969
Albania	1944	Angola	1975
Kurile Islands	1945	Madagascar	1975
North Korea	1945	Laos	1975
Carpatho Ukraine	1945	South Vietnam	1975
Yugoslavia	1945	Ethiopia	1977
Tannu Tuva	1945	Mozambique	1977
Bulgaria	1946	Afghanistan	1978–79
Hungary	1947	Cambodia*	1979
Poland	1947	Grenada	1979
Romania	1947	Zimbabwe (Rhodesia)**	1980
Czechoslovakia	1948		

*Cambodia fell to Chinese-backed communists in 1975; Russian-backed communists from Vietnam took control of Cambodia in 1979.

**Although Zimbabwe (formerly Rhodesia) is not considered to be a communist nation, its leader, Robert Mugabe, is a devoted Marxist.

This chart does not include the substantial number of nations which are allied with the Soviet Union but are not officially "communist." These nations include the Congo, Mali, Syria, Guinea-Bissau and Libya, among others.

War II. In 1945, a conference was held by President Roosevelt, British Prime Minister Winston Churchill and Soviet Premier Josef Stalin at Yalta.

Soviet dissident Alexander Solzhenitsyn describes what happened at that meeting:

"In order to buy Stalin's friendship at the end of the war, the west turned over 1.5 million people who were then in Allied hands and who did not wish to return to Stalin's tyranny. Among them were entire Russian divisions, Tartars and Caucasian batallions, as well as prisoners of war and forced laborers numbering in the hundreds of thousands, including old men, women and children. Stalin manipulated Roosevelt with ease, effortlessly assuring himself of control over eastern Europe."[2]

So while the rest of the world lay down its weapons after World War II, Russia began arming itself to the teeth. The Soviets exploited every opportunity to invade or foment revolution in other countries.

THE IRON CURTAIN FALLS

By the end of 1946, Winston Churchill, recognizing the alarming signs, gave his famous "Iron Curtain" speech decrying Soviet expansionism.

(An isolated incident just after World War II illustrated just how easily the U.S. could have clamped down on Soviet expansion. In 1946, Russian troops invaded Iran. President Truman summoned then-Soviet ambassador to the U.S. Andrei Gromyko into the White House. As Senator Henry Jackson reported the meeting, Truman told Gromyko flatly: Soviet troops should evacuate Iran within 48 hours—or the U.S. would use the atomic bomb, which it alone possessed. " 'We're going to drop it on you,' " Jackson quoted Truman as telling the Russian. "They moved in 24 hours," Jackson added.)[3]

HISTORY TEACHES
THAT MAN LEARNS NOTHING
FROM HISTORY

Attempts to appease aggressors have never once worked. They only encourage the aggressors to reach for more. The longer free people put off a showdown with a nation bent on conquest, the stronger their enemy becomes.

British ambassador Neville Chamberlain tried to appease Hitler at Munich in 1939. We know now that if the Allied nations had gotten tough and confronted Hitler, he could never have started World War II.

Crazy as it may have sounded to many at the time, U.S. General George Patton warned us of the danger of communism at the end of World War II. Patton wanted to attack the Soviets and liberate the Russian people from communist domination. Some people may think Patton harsh. But had the U.S. taken his advice it surely wouldn't be in the mess it is in today.

Even at this late hour, we should remember the words of General Douglas MacArthur, who said, "Timidity breeds conflict, and courage often prevents it. Never enter a conflict unless you are committed to victory."

DOMINOES ANYONE?

After the Korean war ended (an unresolved ending), the communist regimes in Russia and China stepped up their meddling in southeast Asia. As in Korea, the conflicts in Vietnam were never resolved. Now all of southeast Asia, except for Thailand, belongs to the communists. And I predict that lone holdout will soon be lost.

In the '60s and '70s, we were assured by the anti-Vietnam War protest movement that there was absolutely no truth to the "Domino Theory." Those protesters were wrong.

Closer to home, the U.S. allowed the communist takeover of Cuba to succeed, giving the Russians a base from which to spread revolution throughout Latin America.

At the time, we were assured by *New York Times* correspondent Herbert L. Matthews that Fidel Castro was a "peasant patriot, a strong anti-communist and a Robin Hood defender of the people."[4] Then-senator John F. Kennedy likened Castro to the great South American patriot Simon Bolivar.

Our attitudes then made a confrontation like the Cuban missile crisis inevitable. Today, there are Soviet missiles and combat troops just 90 miles from U.S. soil.

WHY HAS RUSSIA SUCCEEDED?

Communism has spread from the Soviet Union to enslave about 2 billion people today. The Russians are on the offensive like never before, as evidenced by the recent invasion of Afghanistan.

Why is this allowed to happen?

One reason is that we have swallowed Russian propaganda. U.S. Senator William Fulbright once said, "The only alternative to our present policy of compromise and accommodation is nuclear war."

But another senator, Barry Goldwater, correctly surmised: "This is precisely the propaganda line the communists have been pushing since they exploded their first atomic device."

In reality, the Russians don't want nuclear war any more than we do. But they have pushed "brinkmanship" in order to paralyze any opposition to their continual conquests and revolutions.

Solzhenitsyn seems to have correctly analyzed the U.S.'s failure to admit the truth about communism. He said: "All warnings to the west about the pitiless and insatiable nature of communist regimes have proved to be in vain because the acceptance of such a view would be too terrifying. For decades it has been standard practice to deny reality by citing 'peaceful coexistence,' 'detente' and 'the Kremlin leadership's pursuit of peace.' Meanwhile, communism envelopes country after country and achieves new missile capabilities."[5]

THE FATAL SALT SYNDROME

Because U.S. administrations from Kennedy to Carter have followed the McNamara theory—namely that the Russians really want peace and will disarm if America does so first—the U.S.'s very survival is now in mortal danger.

Just look at the chart which compares weapon strengths of the U.S. and the U.S.S.R. In every significant area, the Russians have gained the lead and are pulling away.

As the Biblical prophets predicted long ago, the Russians now possess a "splendidly equipped" army. In fact, the Russian military is the most destructive war machine ever assembled. And they achieved this status while supposedly bound by a solemn treaty to "limit the construction and deployment of strategic weapons" (the SALT agreement).

WHO'S ON WHOSE SIDE?

A recent revelation dumbfounded me. According to an article in *Time* magazine, western technology has helped develop the terrifying military power of the communist world.

One example of this is the Kama River truck factory recently built in Russia. Two U.S. financial institutions, the Chase Manhattan Bank and the Export-Import Bank, put up 90 percent of the $2 billion loan needed to construct the plant. Those loans are guaranteed by the U.S. government. Should the Russians decide not to pay back the loans, *our* taxes will pay off *their* debts!

The facility has the world's largest industrial computer system, thanks to U.S. technology. The plant can produce between 150,000 and 200,000 vehicles annually, anything from military scout cars to tanks to troop carriers to rocket launchers.

KAMA RIVER TRUCKS

The insanity of our involvement in building this facility was pointed out by a recent disclosure. U.S. defense department officials have known for three years that military vehicles were being produced at the Kama River facility. In fact, the plant turned out trucks used during the recent invasion of Afghanistan, a defense department spokesman revealed.

Before the plant was built, some Pentagon officials urged that the U.S. refuse to help construct it. According to the defense department source, the U.S. state department overruled those objections. The benefit to detente, they decided, was "well worth the risk."[6]

An American government official recently visited the Kama River plant. He reports that V-12 diesel engines were being made there.

"There is only one vehicle in Russia that uses that type of engine," the official said, "and that's a Russian battle tank."

In light of the fact that the Soviets already have a nine to one advantage over the U.S. in the front-line battle tank department, it seems that the Kama River plant investment was a very dumb risk.

A COUPLE OF PARTING SHOTS

In carefully researching this chapter, one thing came through with sickening clarity: The foreign policies of the western nations, especially the U.S., have done more to aid the tremendous buildup of Soviet power than has any other single factor. Whatever the motives were, the facts speak for themselves.

The most important lesson to be learned from this chapter, however, is this: The Soviet Union and its satellites have now reached the position of military superiority and strategic world power to fulfill their predicted dreadful role in history.

The pages of Ezekiel's and Daniel's prophecies are beginning to look like today's headlines.

SEVEN
KINGS OF THE EAST

"Political power comes out of the barrel of a gun, The gun must never slip from the grasp of the Chinese communist party."

—Mao Tse-tung

"In fear of the Soviet Union, the United States finds communist China as an ally. China will help you defeat the Soviets, but after that, no power on Earth will keep China from world conquest."

—Alexander Solzhenitsyn

China has a momentous—and terrifying—place in the prophetic picture of the last days.

As was noted in *The Late Great Planet Earth*, the Book of Revelation (chapter 16, verse 12) predicts that "the Kings of the East" will move across the Euphrates River, the ancient boundary between the Middle East and the Orient, and travel southwest into the war that will rage around Israel. According to prophecy, this Asian army will number 200 million soldiers (Revelation 9:13–19).

THE 20TH CENTURY VIEWED FROM THE 1ST

The Apostle John, who experienced the vision of this war in the 1st century, tried to describe the vehicles which carried this great army. All this 1st century man knew of soldier transport was the use of horses. It's obvious, however, that the description he gave was not that of a real horse.

To his primitive eye, the beasts looked like lions wearing armored breastplates. They spit something like fire from their mouths. I believe this 1st century prophet saw 20th century battle tanks or armored personnel carriers. And I believe John was forecasting an armed invasion of the Middle East by communist China and its Asian allies.

According to this terrifying prophecy, here's how this invasion will take place:

"The King of the North (Russia) will come to his end in Israel, and no one will help him" (Daniel 11:45). Ezekiel also predicts that the Russian army will be destroyed in the Middle East, and their homeland will become "a lake of fire" (Ezekiel 38:14–39:6).

Who will deal the Russians this fatal blow? The Bible isn't clear whether a supernatural power or combined Chinese and western forces will defeat the Soviets. My opinion, which I will discuss later in this chapter, is that China and possibly the U.S. and their allies will wipe out the Soviet army. But China won't be satisfied with that victory.

Instead, the Chinese, in their quest to conquer the world, will turn and destroy one-third of its population in the final great war known as Armageddon. The Chinese will use weapons which give off fire, brimstone and smoke, according to John. I believe his vision depicted nuclear bombs, which spew fire, molten substances and radioactive clouds.

CHINA'S ROAD TO ARMAGEDDON

In this chapter I will trace how historical events have been moving in precisely the direction the prophets predicted for China.

It is amazing to see the changes in China since the beginning of this century. Back then, China didn't display any hint of becoming the superpower of the end-time prophetic scenario. The country was ruled by feudal landlords at odds with one another, and there was no strong central government.

The Chinese character was pacifist, in keeping with its Confucian religious ideal. The war-making tendency was almost nonexistent. The Chinese were isolated from the great industrial revolution then sweeping through the western world.

The leadership of Chan So Lin, at the beginning of this century, produced the first successful move toward uniting the factious warlords of China. Later, Chiang Kai-shek continued this movement.

But the most important force to prepare China for its prophetic role was communism.

When Mao Tse-tung led 100,000 Chinese communist rebels on the famous "Long March" of 1934, a desperate civil war erupted. Mao's forces fought relentlessly against the army of Chiang Kai-shek.

As was noted in chapter six, the U.S. handed China over to the communists by withdrawing military support from Chiang when he refused to form a coalition government with Mao.

U.S. Senator Barry Goldwater, in his book *With No Apologies*, had this to say about our betrayal of China: "We were told that Chou En-Lai and Mao Tse-tung were amiable, benevolent reformers determined to free the Chinese people from the oppressive, corrupt government of Chiang Kai-shek. General George Marshall ordered Chiang to admit Chou and Mao into a coalition government. When Chiang refused, we withdrew American logistic support. Chiang was forced to flee to Formosa, and Mainland China came under communist rule. The agrarian reformers, Mao and Chou, executed at least 50 million Chinese who refused to cooperate."

In order to unify the Chinese people, Mao had to smash their historical cultural and religious beliefs with his so-called "Cultural Revolution." The pacifist nature of Confucianism had to be replaced with a determined militarism.

MacARTHUR VS. THE CHINESE

Mao formally proclaimed the birth of the "People's Republic of China" on Oct. 1, 1949. Just one year later, the Chinese were aiding the communist North Korean forces which invaded South Korea.

It was then that the U.S. established its "no-win" war policy in Asia. The Chinese communists were allowed to have a sanctuary north of the Yalu River, a post from which they sent waves of soldiers and weapons against the outnumbered Allied troops to the south. When President Truman adopted this policy he guaranteed an eventual war with the communists in southeast Asia. Probably, there will be another war in Korea because of our indecisive actions there 30 years ago.

U.S. General Douglas MacArthur protested Truman's decision so strenuously that the President took away the general's command. In a 1951 speech before Congress, MacArthur noted the dramatic change Mao had wrought in the Chinese people:

"The Chinese people have become thus militarized in their concepts and their ideals. They now constitute excellent soldiers with competent staffs and commanders. This has produced a new and dominant power in Asia, which in its own concepts and methods has become aggressively imperialistic with a lust for expansion and increased power normal to this type of imperialism."

MacArthur also warned of the folly of our policy toward China: "There are some who for various reasons would appease Red China. They are blind to history's clear lesson. For history teaches, with unmistakable emphasis, that appeasement but begats new and bloodier war. It (history) points to no single instance where the end has justified that means— where appeasement has led to more than a sham peace. Like blackmail, it lays the basis for new and successively greater demands until, as in blackmail, violence becomes the only alternative. Why, my soldiers asked me, should we surrender military advantages to an enemy in the field? I could not answer.

"Some may say it is to avoid spread of conflict into an all-out war with China; others, to avoid Soviet intervention. Neither explanation seems valid.

"For China is already engaging with the maximum power it can commit and the Soviets will not necessarily mesh their actions with our moves.

"Like a cobra, any new enemy will more likely strike whenever it feels that the relativity in military or other potential is in its favor on a world-wide basis."

Before Truman recalled him, General MacArthur mapped out a strategy which, if used, could have destroyed Red China's power to fight wars for the rest of this century. The plan called for a land attack on the communists by Chiang Kaishek's Formosa-based army, aided by U.S. bombardment from the sea and the air. At that time, we were the only country with the atomic bomb, so there was no chance that Russia would have interfered. Instead, we allowed the Chinese to increase their influence—and their confidence.

CHINA'S DRIVE TO POWER

Buoyed by their negotiating triumph in North Korea, China began demonstrating to the world that it could overcome its late start in the technology race. Just two and a half years after testing a crude atomic bomb, China shocked the world by detonating an H-bomb. During the '70s, the Chinese built ballistic missiles capable of delivering nuclear warheads on most of Asia and parts of Europe.

But China's leaders realized their nation could never become a true world power without technology and economic aid from the west. The Chinese also feared that a hostile Russia on its border would soon surround China with weapons at the ready unless the U.S. could be persuaded to beef up its western Pacific forces.

HOW PING-PONG CHANGED HISTORY

In April of 1971, the Red Chinese made their move by inviting a U.S. table tennis team accompanied by journalists to tour their country. We immediately snapped at the bait and began sending a steady stream of newsmen, businessmen and politicians to China's welcoming shores. These visits generated valuable propaganda for China, spreading the word of the new conditions and attitudes there.

Peking climaxed the strategy by inviting President Nixon for a visit in 1971. A year later, the U.S. embargo against trade with communist China was lifted.

The next major step was taken by President Carter in 1978. He approved sending U.S. technology and turnkey industrial facilities to the Chinese. These favors were granted under the naive notion that nothing of a strategic nature was being given away.

WE NEVER LEARN

Will the U.S. never learn? To a communist military state bent on world conquest, nothing lacks strategic value. Even food is strategic, because a gift of grain frees farm employees to work in factories building war machines.

Automotive factories are also strategic, as we learned from the Kama River plant we helped build in the Soviet Union. The Chinese will not build luxury automobiles in the factories we are constructing there. No! They will turn out trucks and armored personnel carriers to rapidly move their soldiers into war.

The computers and other technology we are sending the Chinese will be copied and used to make sophisticated weapons that will one day be turned on us.

In fact, since the Soviets invaded Afghanistan, we have begun sending arms to the Chinese. The thinking behind this move seems to be sensible at first glance. Supporters say the only way we can counter Russia's massive military strength is to make China strong. This would divert Russian troops to protect the border the Soviet Union shares with China.

That is the essence of "detente": Play one enemy against

another to prevent either's full might from being used against the U.S. and our allies.

ANOTHER FATAL MISCALCULATION?

Alexander Solzhenitsyn, who understands communism as well as anyone alive, made this comment about our stance toward China: "In expectation of World War III, the West again seeks cover, and finds Communist China an ally! This is another betrayal, not only of Taiwan, but of the entire oppressed Chinese people. Moreover, it is a mad, suicidal policy: Having supplied billion-strong China with American arms, the west will defeat the U.S.S.R., but thereafter no force on earth will restrain communist China from world conquest."[1]

Solzhenitsyn echoes the Biblical prophets, who said that the Oriental people, led by China, will battle the western nations in the planet's last great war. So it is plain to see that the arms we are now sending the Chinese will be turned against us after the Russians are destroyed in the Middle East (see chapter 12 of *The Late Great Planet Earth* for details about this war).

COMMUNISM IS COMMUNISM, NO MATTER *WHO* IT ENSLAVES

Our leaders' idea that one form of communism (Chinese) is good and another (Russian) is bad is the height of folly and misunderstanding. Yet our foreign policy planners continue to act on that theory. Their racist notion claims that Soviet communism is brutal because of the nature of the Russian people. That type of thinking ignores history.

Solzhenitsyn correctly observed: "Communism can implement is 'ideals' only by destroying the core and foundation of a nation's life. He who understands this will not for a minute believe that Chinese communism is more peace-loving than the Soviet variety (it is simply that its teeth have not yet grown) or that Marshall Tito's brand is kindly by nature. The latter was also leavened with blood, and it too consolidated its power by mass killings."[2]

As an American, it makes me sad to see my country help the Chinese prepare for their role in the last awful war. But as one who believes absolutely in what the Hebrew prophets have predicted, it makes me alert with excitement, for I know that the time of Jesus the Messiah's return must be very near.

EIGHT
THE ROMAN EMPIRE— PHASE II

"As long as Europe remains politically divided, it is no match for the Soviet Union. Europe must unite."

—Jean Monet of France, a founder of the European Common Market

During the last three-and-a-half years of the world as we know it, the final great war will rage. As I've mentioned many times, this war will climax with a holocaust that will wipe nearly all human life off the planet. Only an awesome intervention will prevent Earth's total destruction.

According to the Bible's prophets, the Messiah, Jesus of Nazareth will return and save the world. He will then judge those who have brought such ruin upon the world and its people. All those who survive the holocaust and have already accepted God's gift of reconciliation will go into a completely restored new world. This new world is discussed more fully in two of my previous books, *The Late Great Planet Earth* and *There's a New World Coming.* I'll talk more about this later.

The prophets also had a prediction for the period leading up to the last great war. This prophecy, among the most detailed in the Bible, tells us that a great political and economic power will rise in western Europe. This power, composed of 10 separate "kingdoms" united in the final days, will be led by the "anti-Christ."

This charismatic leader, who will receive his powers from Satan himself, will appear to devote his life to world peace. But in reality, he will lead us to the final holocaust.

Let's examine the many prophecies which warn us about the great European power and its evil leader.

DANIEL'S PREVIEW OF WORLD EMPIRES

The prophet Daniel forecast each successive empire which would rule the world, from his own time until the end of history. The first empire, which ruled during Daniel's lifetime, was Babylon.

Daniel predicted that Medes and Persia would combine to conquer Babylon. He also predicted that Medes would rule the new empire first, and then the Persians would dominate (Daniel 8:3, 20).

Against incredible odds, the combined Medes-Persia army conquered Babylon around 530 B.C. The new empire's king was Darius the Mede. After his reign, the Persians ruled—an exact fulfillment.

THE GREEK EMPIRE

Daniel forecast that the Greeks would then conquer the Persians (Daniel 8:5–8 and 21–22). He made this prediction during the reign of Babylonian king Balshazzar, before the Persians had defeated Babylon.

Daniel said the Greeks would be victorious because of the genius of their first king.

Two hundred years after Daniel spoke, a young Macedonian genius who had been taught by Aristotle united all five tribes of Greece—something no one else was able to do. His name was Alexander, known as Alexander the Great.

Young Alexander developed a new battle formation, the phalanx. Fighting at the head of his army, he used this new formation to defeat the Persians, even though the Greeks were outnumbered by about 20 to one.

Daniel's prophecy continued: "Then the male goat

(Greece) magnified himself exceedingly. But as soon as he was mighty, the large horn (Alexander) was broken; and in its place there came up four conspicuous horns toward the four winds of heaven" (Daniel 8:8).

The prophet explained his vision: "The shaggy goat represents the kingdom of Greece, and the large horn that is between his eyes is the first king. The broken horn and the four horns that arose in its place represent four kingdoms which will arise from his nation, although not with his power."

How did Daniel's prophecy fare? Having conquered all that was worth conquering, Alexander died prematurely of boredom and alcoholism at age 33 in Persia. As he lay dying, his generals asked to whom he bequeathed his empire. They expected Alexander to will it to his son.

Instead, Alexander broke tradition and said, "Give it to the strongest." Whereupon his four top generals, Lysymmacus, Casander, Selecus and Ptolemy, divided the Greek empire amongst themselves. But the four parts divided never held the power that unified Greece did under Alexander.

Thus was Daniel's prophecy fulfilled to the letter.

THE ROMAN EMPIRE—PHASE I

It is generally accepted that around 68 B.C., 400 years after Alexander's reign, the Romans conquered what was left of the Greek empire. Rome expanded to form the greatest world empire in history.

But that empire began to crumble and decay from within. Although bands of barbarians fought with Roman armies for centuries, no external power ever succeeded in destroying the empire. In the end, Rome fell apart and was divided into lesser powers. Rome's legacy was a religious empire, which exists to this day.

Ever since Rome fell, many men have tried to put the Roman empire back together. Charlemagne tried and failed in the 8th century. The Moslems made an attempt to reunite the empire with no success. Efforts were also made by the

Austrian Hapsburg dynasty, Napoleon, and Kaiser (the German equivalent of Caesar) Wilhelm.

Adolf Hitler proclaimed that he would consolidate all of Europe, and that his empire would last for 1,000 years. He too was crushed.

WHAT ARMIES COULDN'T DO, ECONOMICS CAN

Despite all these failures to form another Roman empire, we know that a rebirth will occur. Daniel predicted that during the last days a ten-nation confederacy will rise up from the remains of the old Roman Empire.

Here are Daniel's words: "Thus He said: 'The fourth beast will be a fourth kingdom on the Earth (phase I of the Roman Empire), which will be different from all other kingdoms, and it will devour the whole Earth and tread it down and crush it" (Daniel 7:23).

The above prophecy refers to the first Roman empire. In the next verse, Daniel says: "And as for the ten horns, out of this kingdom (ancient Rome) ten kings (or kingdoms) will arise . . ." (Daniel 7:24 NASB).

So this second form of Rome, the fourth kingdom, will have "10 kingdoms or nations" which will band together.

The remainder of the prophecy says that this new Roman empire will rise up during the final days of history, and God's anointed kin, the Messiah, will destroy it and establish God's kingdom in its place (Daniel 7:26-28).

Daniel's prophecy anticipated a long gap between the ancient and the 10-nation phases of the Roman Empire. His prediction also made it clear that no other power would dominate the world's final days.

Since Rome first fell, many nations have tried to build similar empires, though none has yet succeeded. Today, those who can see what is happening in the world feel sure that Soviet-backed communism is on its way to world domination. I would hold that belief myself—if I didn't know the

Bible's prophecy about this confederacy of the ten nations. Still, there are some logical questions to be asked:

- How will the nations of western Europe unite and form a new world empire when so many others have tried and failed?

- How will Europe take leadership of the west away from the U.S. which has dominated it for 40 years?

- How will this ten-nation power stop the Russian bear's headlong push toward world enslavement?

THE RISE OF THE ROMAN EMPIRE II

In 1969, I wrote in *The Late Great Planet Earth* that I, along with many other Bible students, believed that the European Economic Community (EEC or "Common Market") was the beginning of the revised form of the Roman Empire predicted in the Bible.

At that time, there were only six nations (France, West Germany, the Netherlands, Belgium, Luxembourg and Italy) in the association. Yet I believed emphatically that certain facts about the EEC's origin and purpose indicated that this fledgling group would fulfill the prophecies of Daniel and the Book of Revelation. Here are some of the facts, as I saw them:

- The EEC was born with the signing of a treaty in 1957 in Rome. According to the prophecies in Revelation chapter 17, verses 9 and 18, Rome will be the capital of the 10-nation federation. Since the treaty was signed there, Rome has a strong case for becoming the political capital.

- The visionaries who founded the EEC expressed their ultimate goal right from the start. Men such as France's Robert Schumann and Jean Monet (called the "father" of the EEC) and Germany's Dr. Walter Hallstein all spoke of three stages of the EEC's evolution. The first stage was the elimination of trade barriers such as tariffs and import quotas, to increase mobility of capital and labor among member nations. The second stage was the formation of a full economic union with a common currency. The final stage would be a political confederation, thus creating the United States of Europe.

So the ultimate goal has always been to create a political union of the so-called inner member nations. I stress "inner" because there are also cooperating members of the EEC which are not considered part of the political group.

• The target number of member nations was set at 10. I was privileged to serve as a photographer and researcher for a reporter who was chosen by the U.S. State Department to attend a briefing on the EEC in Brussels. At that briefing, a high-level spokesman for the EEC said several times that the ultimate political union would be composed of "10 nations."

That 10 nation goal was repeated in a *Time* magazine article titled, "Europe's Dreams of Unity Revive." That article said, "Should all go according to the most optimistic schedules, the Common Market could someday expand into a 10-nation economic entity whose industrial might would far surpass that of the Soviet Union."[1]

(It is possible that *more* than 10 nations could at one point be admitted. But in the final stages, it will number 10.)

• From the very beginning, it was clear that the EEC's main source of power would come from trade and economics. This fact fit in with another prophecy concerning the revived Roman Empire. I first read this prediction in the early sixties, while studying the Bible's forecast of the destruction of the 10-nation confederacy (Revelation 18:11–18). The "merchants of the Earth" cry loudest when this empire falls, because it had brought "material benefit" to the whole world. That indicates to me that this empire will be an enormous industrial power with an incredible network of world trade. This is exactly what the EEC is becoming.

The average person doesn't realize the potential power of a politically-united EEC. But consider a few facts with me.

Today, even a divided EEC is a great power. According to

U.S. News and World Report, "On paper, the Common Market seems to be an economic giant with productive capacity close to equalling that of the United States. In 1978, its 260 million people turned out $1.94 trillion in goods and services, compared to $2.1 trillion for the U.S. Its exports outstrip America's by more than 50 percent. It accounts for 21 percent of the world's production and 35 percent of trade."[2]

This kind of clout is even more amazing when you consider the political, social and economic divisions which at times have the EEC member nations moving at cross purposes. But the potential of the united EEC is awesome. The output of a single unit would be far more powerful than merely adding the outputs of the individual nations. Unification would multiply the members' strength.

To illustrate this, imagine that General Motors, the Ford Motor Company, American Motors and Chrysler Corporation all merged. The power of the whole corporation would be far greater than just the sum of its parts. And so it would be with a united EEC.

When it forms a political union, the potential of the EEC's economic, political and military might will be awesome. And that power is exactly as the prophets said it would be.

But there's one missing part. The confederacy needs a great leader to bring it together and harness its potential. Both the current political reality and the words of the prophets show us the necessity of a charismatic, dynamic leader.

As I will discuss later in this chapter, this leader, known in the Bible as the "anti-Christ," will drive the 10-nation confederacy to its place as the world's greatest power.

TEN YEARS LATER

Major changes have occurred in the Common Market since I wrote *The Late Great Planet Earth*. In that book, I wrote: "As the U.S. loses power, western Europe will be forced to unite and become the standard-bearer of the western world. Look for the emergence of a 'United States of Europe,' composed of 10 member nations." Here's a list of some of the changes:

• January 1, 1973: The United Kingdom, Ireland and Denmark officially joined the EEC, and the "community of nine" came into existence.

• 1979: Greece was accepted as the 10th member of the EEC. Ratification, a formality, is set for January 1, 1981.

• July 17, 1979: A landmark event occurred on this day. To the untrained eye, it may have seemed insignificant. But on that day, the first EEC parliament was formed, made up of 410 delegates elected directly by the voters.

What an amazing recovery Europe has made. Just 34 years after World War II reduced it to ruins, the continent was on its way to unification. Ironically, the parliament's first president is a French Jewess, Simone Weil, a survivor of Hitler's death camps.

"Turning points in history have a way of slipping by unnoticed," *Time* magazine commented in an article on the formation of the EEC parliament. But some of Europe's most powerful men were elected as delegates to the body. "We shall have the big stars of European politics in the parliament," France's Edgard Pisani told *Time*. "That is one reason why this parliament can have great political influence."[3]

I believe that this parliament, though currently limited in power, will be the framework for the political force which will be headed by the anti-Christ. And I believe that leader is alive somewhere in Europe; perhaps he is already a member of the EEC parliament.

THE EEC'S PROPHETIC COUNTDOWN NEARS THE FINISH

Recent world events are pushing the EEC down the path toward a strong political union. On April 15, 1980, the U.S.

told NATO and our western European allies that because of the Russian threat to Iran and the important Persian Gulf area, all our available forces would have to be centered in that part of the world. Therefore, western Europe was going to have to begin shouldering most of its defense burden.

I knew this would happen. I wrote in *The Late Great Planet Earth* that ". . . as the United States loses power, western Europe will be forced to unite and become the standard-bearer." It appears that the U.S. is now a second-class military power, and we can no longer challenge Russia in each troubled area.

This became painfully evident during Russia's recent uncontested invasion of Afghanistan. According to an article in the *Los Angeles Times*, "A few sources believe that another perception of the Kremlin is that the U.S. has become a second-class power, with severe economic problems at home and weakening alliances abroad, as a nation lacking the ability and the political will to exert its influence on this side of the world."[4]

For some time, Europe has questioned America's resolve in facing up to Russia. Now the NATO countries must build up their own defensive capabilities. I have long said that the Soviet communist threat would someday be the catalyst needed to form a United States of Europe.

A well-informed military expert told me that right now, NATO would be so hopelessly outnumbered in a conventional war with Russia that the communists could push European forces all the way to the English Channel in a matter of weeks.

WHY EUROPE LOSES TRUST

The only hope for stopping a Russian sweep through Europe would be a strong nuclear force at the ready. But that hope was scuttled when President Carter changed his plans for deploying the neutron bomb in Europe. This move especially dismayed West German president Helmut Schmidt, who put his political career in jeopardy by urging European acceptance of the neutron bomb.

(Carter changed his original decision to deploy the neutron bomb system because the Soviets were threatening to back out of the SALT II talks. Oh, that they would do us such a favor!)

When General Alexander Haig resigned his command of NATO, he said, "We are now clearly fundamentally deficient in theater (tactical) nuclear capability. The area of great concern is the longer and middle range capability; the area which involves NATO counters to Soviet SS-20 missiles and the (supersonic) Backfire bombers."[5]

The NATO and EEC members have begun to feel isolated and deserted by the U.S. in the face of the ever-increasing Soviet threat on their doorsteps. Our European allies feel that the SALT agreements have actually threatened their defenses, since the treaties only deal with long-range nuclear missiles.

Their point is well taken: The SALT talks intentionally ignored the build-up of Soviet middle-range ballistic missiles and the new supersonic "Backfire" bomber airplanes. French general Pierre Gollois said, "I question the usefulness of SALT to Europe when, in fact, the reverse may be true. It is a position of potential superiority for the Soviet Union which is endangering the cohesiveness of NATO."[6]

WHAT MUST BE WILL BE

From the standpoint of prophecy, this threat to Europe had to arise. The EEC must be forced to unite and become a dominant power. It must somehow tap its vast potential to stop the Soviet drive toward world domination.

Events in Europe have just about reached the stage where the real key to the revived Roman empire, the anti-Christ, must come forward.

According to Revelation, chapter 13, verses 1 through 10, this leader will be relatively obscure at first. Then, he will receive a mortal head wound, possibly from a bullet.

Miraculously, he will be raised back to life and restored to good health. It will not be God who saves him, however. This miracle will belong to Satan.

POSSESSED AND LOOKING GOOD

This man will sell his soul to gain power over the world, and Satan will possess him completely. Satan, whom the Bible called the most powerful, intelligent and beautiful creature God ever made, will devote all of his powers to the anti-Christ.

After he recovers from his head wound, Satan takes him over, and gives this man superhuman psychic powers, brilliance, and strong personal magnetism. He will immediately rise to prominence in the EEC and from that post he will offer the world amazing solutions to all its complex and terrifying problems.

The anti-Christ will be an electrifying, spellbinding public speaker. He will also be an unmatched negotiator. He will even have the power to mesmerize and charm the Russians.

Because of his superhuman powers and his solutions to the world's conflicts, the anti-Christ will be chosen to lead the EEC. However, three of the member nations will refuse to relinquish their sovereignty to him, and he will overthrow their governments by force (Daniel 7:8 and 24).

Apparently, he will achieve great personal power within the EEC because of his plan to eliminate the threat of a greatly-feared world war. The prophet Daniel said of him, "And through his shrewdness he will cause deceit to succeed . . . he will destroy many by means of peace." (Daniel 8:25 Literal Translation).

THE ANTI-CHRIST'S PROPHET

The anti-Christ will achieve the top spot in Europe on the strength of his own personality. But he will need the help of the Jewish false prophet mentioned in Revelation chapter 13, verses 11 through 17, to gain domination over the entire world.

The prophet too will have the power to work miracles, and he will use that power to convince the world—and in particular, the Jews—to worship the anti-Christ. In return for their devotion, the anti-Christ will promise the Israelis protection, and the right to use the Temple mount in Old Jerusalem for purposes of worship (Daniel 9:27).

The anti-Christ will then spread his power throughout the world by devising an ingenious economic program. His 10-nation base of power will be the center of a trade network which will involve every nation on the face of the Earth.

HOW NUMBERS MAKE A WORLD RULER

Once that network is established, the false prophet will take it a step further. He will limit membership in the trade network to those citizens alone who worship the anti-Christ. Those worshipers will each be assigned a trade number. Without that number, no one will be permitted to buy or sell anything (Revelation 13:16–17).

SOME IMPORTANT DEDUCTIONS

The prophecies concerning the anti-Christ and the false prophet give us some insight as to what world conditions must soon exist. First, there must be a shift of power to western Europe. Second, there must be a centralization of economic power. This second condition requires that the world's monetary systems be united into one system. It implies a "currency-less" form of exchange.

COMPUTERS IN PROPHECY

As scary as it may sound, many of these conditions are already coming to pass. At least one of these conditions would have been impossible before the advent of computers.

An international currency has already been introduced. Units called "special drawing rights," or SDRs, are the currency which member nations of the International Monetary Fund currently exchange.

But even closer to the prophecy of a world currency system is the use of "electronic funds transfer," or EFT. This system eliminates the need for cash by electronically adding or subtracting money from a person's account as that person earns or spends money. All transactions are conducted using credit cards.

Although this system is still far from being widely used, it is being tested in cities such as Arlington, Ohio, where people for a period were assigned credit cards in place of cash.

I believe that one day soon, currency will no longer be our medium of exchange. Instead, we will all be assigned computer numbers for life.

LET'S PRETEND

Now let's suppose that this system goes into effect. We all have our numbers. It's easy to see how impractical such a system could be, and how insecure it would make us feel. Someone who stole or found your banking card could easily wipe out all of your savings. The only safeguard would be to tattoo the number on your skin with an ink that could be seen only in a special light.

But even with these drawbacks, electronic money would be the most logical, utilitarian and efficient way to trade among people of different lands. There's still one big problem, though: The system puts control of all of the world's assets in one place. The person who controls the main computer controls the world. And that person will be the one who controls the world's trade—the anti-Christ.

THE ONE WHO HAS WISDOM

I believe the scenario just described will happen. The anti-Christ, with the help of his false prophet, will require that a number representing his name become part of your own banking number to make it valid. Revelation chapter 13, verses 17 and 18 says:

"And he (the false prophet) provides that no one should be able to buy or to sell, except the one who has the mark, either the name of the beast (the anti-Christ) or the number of his name.

"There is wisdom. Let him who has understanding calculate the number of the beast, for the number is that of a man; and his number is six hundred and sixty-six."

When the original Greek text of the New Testament was written, each letter of the Greek alphabet had a corresponding number, since the letters were used as numbers also (they didn't have Arabic numerals). So the prophecy says that the anti-Christ's name, translated into Greek and then converted into numbers, should total 666.

We know the anti-Christ's number, but not his name. He will be easily recognized, however. A member of the European Common Market will suffer a head wound which would normally be fatal. Miraculously he will be restored to health. That will be an unmistakable signal.

THE NEW WORLD ORDER

Before I close this chapter on the last great empire, Roman Empire II, I want to mention a prominent group right in this country which is working to reduce our power and establish a world economic and political system.

This prestigious group has already provided the U.S. with many of its top officials, especially in the Department of State. The group has a plan to elevate the EEC to a global economic force and change the currency systems presently in use around the world.

The organization's ultimate goal is to help create a world government which will use economics to rule. The name of the group is the Trilateral Commission, and it is the subject of the next chapter.

NINE
THE NEW
WORLD SYSTEM

"What is now being discussed at the highest levels of government, in both the United States and abroad, is the creation of a new world economic system—a system that will affect jobs in America and elsewhere, the prices consumers pay and the freedom of individuals, corporations and nations to enter into a truly planetary economic system. Indeed, many observers see the advent of the Carter administration and what is now being called the 'Trilateral' cabinet as the harbinger of this new era."

—Jeremiah Novak,
Christian Science Monitor,
Feb. 7, 1977

It amazes me that so few people in the United States have even heard of the Trilateral Commission, much less understand what it is and what it proposes to do.

Since I first heard of this elite group, in 1976, I've asked the many varied audiences to which I've spoken, "How many here today have ever heard of the Trilateral Commission?" Usually just one or two percent of the audience members would raise their hands.

To this day that baffles me. For here is an international group of the western world's most powerful bankers, media leaders, scholars and government officials bent on radically changing the world in which we live, as the quote which introduced this chapter shows.

What this non-elected group is setting out to do—with permission from no one—will indeed affect the individual freedom and economic status of every individual in the world, particularly in the U.S.

SOME DIFFICULT QUESTIONS

For some, this chapter will be difficult to understand. Economics, especially on a world-wide scale, is usually not very

117

interesting to most people (perhaps this is one reason that so few people know of the Trilateral Commission).

But since the Bible predicts the basis of power for the final one-world government, the revived form of the Roman Empire, will be centered around economics and trade, this analysis is absolutely imperative.

Now I want to be clear at the outset: I am not calling the motives of the commission's members evil. So far as I know, the Trilateralist founders and members are convinced they are doing the world a necessary service by bringing stability and order to world trade. The fact that they stand to make some substantial profits and rise to positions of great political power is, I'm sure, considered just rewards for their efforts.

If one doesn't know and believe what God's prophets have forecast about the last stages of history, then there appears to be but one solution for avoiding a holocaust. That solution would be to create some form of a central world government held together by economic interdependence. Creating that form of government seems to be the Trilateral Commission's underlying motive.

THE TRILATERAL WHO?

I'm sure you are wondering by now, "What in the world *is* the Trilateral Commission? Who started it? Who belongs to it? What is its purpose and goals?"

To answer those questions I must go back into history and show the conditions that led to the creation of the commission and why its founders feel it is needed.

FROM EMPIRES TO BRETTON WOODS

There has always been a need for some kind of system to regulate international trade between political powers.

Before World War II, the empires of Britain, Portugal,

France, Holland and the U.S. controlled world trade by posting tariffs to protect their own industries. These tariffs, which are added on to the price of imported goods, made it very difficult for outside nations to trade with countries within the imperial systems.

It became obvious during World War II that the imperial system would not survive in the post-war era. So a pair of brilliant economists, John Maynard Keynes, of Great Britain, and Harry Dexter White, of the U.S., got together to draw up plans for a replacement system. They made these plans in July of 1944 in Bretton Woods, New Hampshire, and the new system took its name from that small town.

THE BRETTON WOODS' PROBLEMS

There were two main problems the Bretton Woods meeting was intended to solve. The first problem was the way nations manipulated their currencies to weaken one another and thus protect their own systems. This practice resulted in worldwide currency instability.

The second problem was the indiscriminate raising of protective tariffs, either by nations or by power blocs. This greatly inhibited free international trade and closed markets to the lesser-developed countries, who already had trouble competing for trade.

THE BRETTON WOODS' SOLUTIONS

To solve the first problem, Bretton Woods proposed setting fixed currency exchange rates. Two international financial institutions, the International Monetary Fund (IMF) and the World Bank, were established for this purpose.

Besides setting currency exchange rates, these institutions would also have the power to provide credit to the world's poorer countries and to lend money to nations ravaged by war.

The new plans would solve the second problem by establishing the "most favored nation" system of trade. Nations which had trouble competing for international business could be granted this special status and thus would be exempt from paying tariffs when they exported goods into other countries. Without the tariffs, these nations would be able to sell their goods more cheaply, and thus stimulate trade.

The international pact which runs this system is called the "General Agreement on Tariffs and Trade," or GATT.

THE BRETTON WOODS' ENFORCER

The whole Bretton Woods system depended upon having a power great enough to enforce the international agreements and discipline nations which violated the rules.

The U.S. was the logical choice for "enforcer." The American dollar was already being used as the basic world currency because it was stable and backed by the gold standard and a healthy economy.

Since the United States consumed more than half the world's total exported goods, it could firmly regulate the "most favored nation" trade system and guarantee all nations fair access to the world markets.

As the world's paramount economic power, the U.S. could also enforce sanctions against violators. The genius of the system was its interlocking set of sanctions. Each part of the plan helped strengthen and enforce the others. For example, if a nation broke the currency manipulation rules, the plan's tariff or loan credit portions could be used to punish.

Though this system had its faults, under it the world enjoyed the greatest expansion in international trade in history. World trade rose from almost zero just after the war to almost $400 billion in 1971.

The Bretton Woods system, instituted after much public debate and with everyone aware of what it would do, greatly encouraged free trade. It made no attempt to tamper with the sovereignty of nations, but rather worked on the basis of a community of sovereign states.

THE FALL OF BRETTON WOODS

Bretton Woods began failing in the early 1960's. That happened mainly because the U.S. could no longer keep stability in the system, nor enforce its rules. The reasons for that were:

• The U.S. dollar lost its stability and power, due to increasing deficits in the country's balance of payments (the value of goods it bought from other nations compared to the value of goods it sold to other nations) and the removal of the gold standard.

• The newly-formed European Common Market and the nation of Japan began offering strong competition in the international marketplace. Their increased consumption of foreign goods meant that the U.S. had less power to exert over violators of the trade agreements.

• The poor Third World countries had to limit the amount of foreign goods they could accept because they couldn't pay for them. According to most observers, the Third World's inability to buy from the developed world's nations was the straw that broke Bretton Woods' back.

According to noted economist and writer Jeremiah Novak, the death of Bretton Woods "was precipitated by the Nixon shocks of 1971, when the United States devalued the dollar and imposed a tariff surcharge on imports."[1]

THE RISE OF THE TRILATERAL COMMISSION

After many unsuccessful efforts by various groups to overhaul the Bretton Woods system it became obvious that something entirely new was needed.

It was in this vacuum that David Rockefeller stepped forth.

He instigated research into the complex problems international affairs faced. Rockefeller picked Columbia University's specialist on international relations, Zbigniew Brzezinski, as the key intellectual who would help him formulate the policies of his new system.

Newsweek decribed the commission's inception: ". . . The Trilateral Commission, a brainchild of David Rockefeller, was transformed into reality by Zbigniew Brzezinski."[2]

According to Senator Barry Goldwater, "Zbigniew Brzezinski and David Rockefeller screened and selected every individual who was invited to participate in shaping and administering the new world order."[3]

The pair attracted some of the keenest minds of Europe, Japan and the U.S. to join their new force.

THE NEW ENFORCER

The commission decided that the core of the new world economic system would be Japan, the European Common Market and the U.S. Those three powers together represented 70 percent of world trade and therefore had the "right and the duty" to create the new system, the commission contended. Collectively, these three powers could enforce the replacement for the Bretton Woods agreements, which the U.S. alone no longer had the power to look after.

This is how the commission got its name; "trilateral" refers to the three spheres of economic power and influence being combined into one force.

One of the new system's keys is that the U.S. must be reduced from its place as leader of the western world.

Jeremiah Novak commented on this: "The group believes that the policies of the trilateral world must be harmonized, as the U.S. alone can no longer take on responsibility for the international economic system. It also believes that if a new order is created, it must be based on a recognition that *the U.S. is now only the first among equals* in the industrial world.

"As a result of this conclusion, *U.S. foreign policy must undergo a transformation of gigantic proportions.*" (All italics mine.)[4]

A WORRISOME ASSUMPTION

This last assumption is what worries many observers. It requires that the U.S. make a deliberate shift in its foreign policies and slip in its prestige so that it no longer is the leader of the western world. To some it appears that steps have already been taken to lower the U.S. power and fit into this new economic mode.

I'll say more on this in a moment, but the lowering of America's power and prestige certainly fits into the prophetic pattern. I wrote in *The Late Great Planet Earth* to expect the U.S. to fade from its position as leader of the Free World and for the Common Market to become the dominant power. The process of transition is evidently here.

A FAR GREATER SCOPE

The areas the Trilateral Commission claims the right to regulate are far greater in scope and magnitude than those covered by Bretton Woods.

According to Novak: "The rules cover such areas as international monetary systems, international trade in raw materials and industrial goods (a new area not covered in Bretton Woods) and use of 'commons,' such as the oceans, space and the (north and south) poles. These rules are seen as universally applicable and subject to sanctions in the event they are violated."[5]

Other new provisions to the system are the need for relationships with communist, Third World and OPEC groups. This system indeed intends to unite the whole world economically.

ECONOMIC ORDER WITHOUT POLITICAL ORDER?

Novak raised a dilemma in his article on the commission: "It is clear that the thinking of the Trilateral Commission goes beyond Bretton Woods and creates an economic reality for which there is no complementary political reality—that is, a world economy without a world government."[6]

It's clear that the Trilateralists do not believe that their new economic order can exist in a political vacuum. Otherwise, why would they have deliberately hand-picked certain members to be trained and groomed for the highest political offices of their home nations?

THE "TRILATERAL ADMINISTRATION"

Nowhere is this Trilateral strategy more evident than in the U.S. According to an article in the *Atlantic Monthly*, "Although the commission's primary concern is economic, the Trilateralists pinpointed a vital political objective: To gain control of the American presidency."[7]

Jimmy Carter, in his first term as Georgia's governor, impressed David Rockefeller by establishing a trade relationship with Japan for his state. Carter also showed an unusual amount of ambition as he sought opportunities to learn foreign policy, and also to meet David Rockefeller.

At this point Carter's ambition matched with the commission's needs. "The founders, anxious to have a liberal Southerner in their ranks, invited Jimmy Carter, then the governor of Georgia, to join them."[8]

Carter became a charter member of the commission in 1973. He received a thorough indoctrination in trilateralist views, particularly on foreign policy, from Brzezinski himself.

There is no question that the commission groomed Carter to be President. He was virtually a political unknown. Yet because of the enormous behind-the-scenes power of the

Trilateralists in the news media, he came from nowhere to capture the White House.

A PACKED OUT HOUSE

As soon as Carter took office, he packed his administration with fellow Trilateralists.

U.S. News and World Report wrote at the time: "The 'Trilateralists' have taken charge of foreign policy-making in the Carter administration, and already the immense power they wield is sparking some controversy. Active or former members of the Trilateral Commission now head every key agency involved in mapping U.S. strategy for dealing with the rest of the world.

"Altogether, 16 high posts in the administration are held by men and women associated with the organization. Some see this concentration of power as a conspiracy at work."[9]

Not only does the commission hold the strings attached to high government officials here, but the same situation exists in Japan and Europe as well. Novak notes, "Its membership roster reads like a Who's Who in business, labor and government."[10]

In this way the commission assures itself of having its plans for a one-world government instituted in the quickest way possible.

HEDGING THE BET

In the 1980 U.S. presidential election, the Trilateralists seem to be hedging their bets. Two potential candidates for the U.S. Presidency, George Bush and John Anderson, are members of the Trilateral Commission. The membership of these prominent men brought the commission considerable national attention, and along with that went several strong blasts of criticism.

It's been interesting to me to watch various news media heavyweights rush to defend the commission against charges that it has gained undue power in the world's governments.

Publications such as the *Wall Street Journal, Time, Newsweek* and *U.S. News and World Report* have all said pretty much the same things. In general, they publish articles which minimize the commission's influence, characterizing its members as a bunch of frustrated and powerless armchair idealists who wish they could institute some of their ideas in world affairs.

Other similar articles call it simply a floating study group with no essential power, and they label the commission's critics as isolationist conservatives or Marxist-leaning leftists.

JUST A THOUGHT

I wonder if the fact that so many news media executives are also commission members has anything to do with these published defenses. The Trilateral Commission's members include men like the editor-in-chief of *Time* magazine, directors of the *New York Times*, the *Wall Street Journal*, the *Los Angeles Times* and the *Washington Post*, and the editorial director of the *Chicago Sun-Times*. [11]

Once again, let me say that I am not questioning the integrity of these men or of any commission members. I'm sure that in their minds they are motivated by a desire to maintain peace and stability in the world.

For the media to say that the Trilateral Commission has no essential political power, however, is an insult to the intelligence of the American public. It also assumes that most Americans didn't read or don't remember the many articles which detailed the commission's growing power and were published in those same newspapers and magazines in the 1977 era.

THE CFR CONNECTION

A world economic system such as the commission is proposing has to be wedded to a similar political point of view. And that political view would have to concentrate mostly on foreign policy.

In 1939, a foreign policy study group made up of specialists in international affairs visited the U.S. state department and offered its services. That group was called the Council on Foreign Relations (CFR).

The Rockefeller Foundation agreed to finance the group's new venture into policy-making. Senator Barry Goldwater reveals: "From that day forward the Council on Foreign Relations has placed its members in policy-making positions with the federal government, not limited to the state department.

"Since 1944 every American Secretary of State, with the exception of James F. Byrnes, has been a member of the CFR.

"I believe the CFR and its ancillary elitist groups are indifferent to communism. They have no ideological anchors. In their pursuit of a new world order they are prepared to deal without prejudice with a communist state, a socialist state, a democratic state, monarchy, oligarchy—it's all the same to them.

"Rear Admiral Chester Ward, of the U.S. Navy (retired), who was a member of the CFR for 16 years, has written, 'The most powerful cliques in these elitist groups have one objective in common—they want to bring about the surrender of the sovereignty and the national independence of the United States.' "[12]

CHECK THE RECORD

Even a casual check of the U.S. foreign policy record reveals one thing clearly: A continuous erosion of American power due to continual concessions to and defeats by the

communist world. With that in mind, remember—the CFR is
the foreign policy precursor of the Trilateral Commission.

THE DANGERS OF TRILATERALISM

The Trilateralists have assumed the right to make changes
of global significance, changes which affect the freedoms of
millions of people. They have done so with no public-
consultation, no debate, no election. They have brought
about these changes in virtual secrecy.

They have set out to capture the highest political offices in
the U.S., Japan and the Common Market countries in order
to make changes in national and international policy. But
they have never informed the people in these countries of
their plans. Along with a growing number of Americans, I
find this inexcusable, arrogant and dangerous.

THE LARGER PICTURE

I believe the Trilateralist movement is unwittingly setting
the stage for the political-economic one-world system the
Bible predicts for the last days. It's happening in concert with
all the other pieces of the prophetic scenario described in this
book.

What the trilateralists are trying to establish will soon be
controlled by the coming world leader—the anti-Christ himself.

TEN
WHAT ABOUT THE U.S.?

"We (the U.S.) are sliding toward a world out of control, with our relative military power declining, with our economical lifeline increasingly vulnerable to blackmail, with hostile radical forces growing in every continent and with the number of countries willing to stake their future on our friendship dwindling."

—former Secretary of State
Henry Kissinger,
Time magazine, April 21, 1980

When discussing the Bible's predictions for the future, the question I am most frequently asked is, "What about the United States—where do we fit into prophecy?"

This isn't an easy question to answer, because there are no specific or even indirect references to America in Bible prophecy.

SOME "KNOWNS"

Though the U.S. itself is not mentioned in the Bible, there are things we do know from which we can make some deductions.

First, prophecy definitely singles out who the leader of the western world will be in the final stage of history—and it *won't* be the U.S. As we have already seen, the 10-nation confederacy that rises up from the ruins of the Old Roman Empire will be the west's dominating power.

The second thing we know is that this "Confederacy of 10," under the leadership of the anti-Christ, will bring all the world's nations under its control for the final period of the present world.

SOME DEDUCTIONS

So from the standpoint of Biblical prophecy, the U.S. *must* fade from its place of leadership for the west and its former supreme superpower status.

There are several possible fates for the U.S. They include:

• A takeover by the communists.

• Destruction by a surprise Soviet nuclear attack (I don't even like to *think* about this possibility).

• Becoming a dependent of the 10-nation European confederacy.

• A far more hopeful fate than any of the above. Let's explore this final possibility.

A RAY OF HOPE

If some critical and difficult choices are made by the American people *right now*, it is possible to see the U.S. remain a world power. We could become an equal ally of the European confederation, with each dependent on the other. In that way, America could keep much of its sovereignty and freedom.

AMERICA AT THE CROSSROADS

Former Secretary of State Henry Kissinger recently spoke out on America's current situation: "I happen to agree with President Carter that the danger to our country is the gravest in the modern period."[1]

Very few Americans realize the enormous multiple dangers that threaten their survival. Even fewer understand how the U.S. got into its perilous predicament. So let's examine the evidence of the U.S.'s present situation, and trace some of the events in history that have brought the situation about.

Now again, I'm not trying to be a political writer. But it is my prayer that enough people will grasp the clear and imminent danger that exists so that some prompt action may be taken.

I don't presume to be wise enough to solve the political aspects of the dilemma. But there are some self-evident courses of action that should be urged.

And above all, there are some spiritual issues which, if recognized, could turn the tide.

As we look at the many crises confronting the U.S., let's also pray for some wise and courageous decisions.

CRISIS OF LEADERSHIP

At the end of World War II, the United States was the most powerful nation on earth. We were the sole possessors of the atomic bomb. We had a clear superiority in the numbers and quality of conventional weapons such as aircraft, naval vessels, tanks and so on. In short, our technological lead and productive capability were unchallenged.

And above all, we had demonstrated the will to sacrifice in order to remain a free society. We had more than just the will to survive: we had the willingness to endure whatever hardships were necessary to survive.

At that high point in power, the U.S., along with the rest of the world, began happily disarming the vast war machine. I should say *almost* the rest of the world, for there was one nation which did not disarm. Rather, that country started a steady buildup of its mighty military machine. That nation was the Soviet Union.

As already documented, every other power came out of World War II with either less territory of the same amount of possessions as when the war started. But the Soviet Union, through clever manipulation of American President Roosevelt at the Yalta conference, had considerably enlarged its empire at the war's end.

Franklin D. Roosevelt was the first U.S. President to make

astonishing concessions to the Russians and misread or refuse to believe their avowed doctrine of world conquest
through "class struggle."

For whatever reasons, Yalta's territorial grants—aided by
America's easygoing attitude—gave the Soviet communists a
stranglehold on the Russian people and a primary power
base for world expansion.

Mao's China—Gift Of U.S.A.

In the late 1940's, the U.S. deliberately withdrew military
support from Chiang Kai-shek's government and allowed
Mao Tse-tung and Chou En-lai to take over mainland China.

U.S. Secretary of State George C. Marshall, a retired U.S.
Army general, advised the American government and people
that Mao and Chou were amiable, benevolent reformers determined to free the Chinese people from the oppressive,
corrupt government of Chiang Kai-shek. Mao and Chou,
Marshall said, were simply agrarian reformers.

Chiang Kai-shek had to flee to the island of Formosa and
set up the free Chinese government of Taiwan when American aid was cut off. The U.S. state department then announced that Formosa and Korea were outside the defense
perimeter of the United States.

Roots Of The Korean War

North Korea was another gift to the Russians courtesy of
F.D.R. The Soviets wasted no time in exporting their communist philosophy and military equipment, which incited
their North Korean satellite to greedily look south to the
non-communist half of Korea.

Right after the U.S. declared Korea outside its "defense
perimeter," the North Koreans, backed by the "amiable"
Mao and his new Chinese communist government, invaded
South Korea.

This turned into one of the bloodiest wars the U.S. has
been involved in. And yet history reveals that American

foreign policy virtually created the climate that allowed that war to erupt.

The Real "Casualty" Of Korea

The Korean conflict finally ended (in 1953), but not without inflicting a major American "casualty." This loss was personified in the firing of U.S. General Douglas MacArthur.

But it went deeper than that. The entire American military establishment was crippled in that war. The administration of Harry Truman ordered the American armed forces to depart from the most fundamental law of warfare—that an army must *win* a war and bring it to as swift an end as possible.

For the politician to tell a military commander that he must fight a war but not win is like telling a preacher that he must preach but not use the Bible nor seek to bring people to faith.

Because the U.S. settled for appeasement, it guaranteed the eventual debacle in Vietnam. It also appears that our indecisive actions then may cause another war in Korea in the near future. Never before in U.S. history had the country refused to pursue victory in battle. The tragedy was compounded by the lengthening of the Korean and Vietnam wars that refusal caused.

That new policy was also responsible for an increase in casualties. The Korean War cost the U.S. 137,051 deaths and injuries. Do we have the right to ask soldiers to sacrifice and risk their lives unless we ourselves are willing to match their risk?

Even more critical, should our soldiers become targets in foreign lands while their government debates the purpose they are there for? Should our military commanders be ordered to fight enemies who are granted—by the U.S. Department of State—special geographical "sanctuaries" from which they can mount attacks?

The Fidel Fiasco

In April of 1957, the *New York Times* published an interview with Cuban rebel Fidel Castro conducted by correspondent Herbert L. Matthews. As was previously mentioned, Matthews brought back a glowing report on Castro's devotion to the Cuban people and his strong anticommunist views.

Senator Barry Goldwater, in his book *With No Apologies*, spelled out the incredible series of events which thereafter put Castro into power in Cuba:

"John Foster Dulles (then Secretary of State) was dying of cancer. Power was exercised by second echelon bureaucrats. These are the career foreign service officers. They are protected in their jobs. Many of them are committed to the 'one-world' concept. Most of them believe the only way to avoid war is to practice a policy of accommodation toward the Russians.

"American ambassador to Cuba Arthur Gardner described Castro as a communist terrorist. *He* (Gardner) *was recalled.*

"Earl E. T. Smith was named to replace him. It is interesting to note that Smith was not permitted to consult with his predecessor (which is a breach of all protocol and practice.)

"Instead, the state department sent him to New York to be briefed by *Times* correspondent Herbert Matthews.

"This failure of the state department to make public Fidel Castro's communist connections is even more difficult to understand when reviewed in conjunction with official reports from Ambassador to Mexico Robert Hill.

"Hill was aware of Castro's participation in Bogota. He repeatedly warned his superiors at (the) State (department) of Castro's close connection with known communist Che Guevara.

"Hill testified under oath, 'Individuals in the Department of State and individuals in the *New York Times* put Castro into power.' "[2]

Cuba Ratified

In the 1962 Cuban crisis, what started out as a bold stand against Soviet introduction of missiles into Cuba wound up as another fiasco.

In order to get the Soviets to agree to remove their missiles from Cuba, President John F. Kennedy guaranteed that the U.S. would not invade or support an invasion of that island country.

Thus a base from which communism could be exported throughout Central and South America was granted safety.

Today, because of that decision, there are missiles, Soviet nuclear submarine bases, military aircraft and Russian combat soldiers just 90 miles away from American soil. And Castro-supported revolutions are raging throughout Central America, around the vital Panama Canal, as well as in far-off Africa.

Cuba is also threatening the waterway access to the entire Caribbean area, by provoking the revolutions which flow from one island to another in that important U.S. sea lane area.

Also, Soviet submarines and aircraft operating from Cuban bases could shut off the vital U.S.-bound oil refined in the Caribbean.

In Africa

U.S. foreign policy supported the communist Patrice Lumumba's overthrow of freedom-loving Moise Tshombe's rule in the Belgian Congo.

In 1961, the U.S. supported the admitted communist Cheddi Jagan takeover of British Guiana.

America backed Kwane Nkrumah, the dictator of Ghana, one of the first of the Soviet satellites in Africa.

In recent times, U.S. and western neglect helped to topple the government of Rhodesia, which fell into the hands of communist rebel Robert Mugabe.

I'm not at all expressing approval for the oppression of blacks by whites. But I don't believe that what is happening in Rhodesia now, for instance, will turn out to be for the betterment of "human rights" for either blacks *or* whites. Zimbabwe, as Rhodesia is now known, will turn into

another freedomless communist state after a short transition
period, mark my words.

This same situation may soon be forced upon the Republic
of South Africa unless some new way of treating that country
is found.

True, the Republic of South Africa's racial apartheid policy
is deplorable. But there must be a way other than forcing the
present government to fail to make the South African nation
acceptable to the world. Otherwise, the U.S. and all the west
will lose a strategic ally that is *absolutely vital* to our survival.

South Africa is our last dependable source of certain
strategic metals that are absolutely necessary to the construction and maintenance of our nuclear and conventional
weapons. If we lose South Africa as a source for these metals,
we will *not* have *any* other source to draw from!

The Iranian Lesson

American foreign policy's bungling and indecision caused
the Shah's government to fall. Although the Shah's rule left
much to be desired, it certainly gave more freedom and stability to the Iranian people than the present chaos does.

Also, the Shah's military was vital to the security of the
Persian Gulf. Now Iran, its people and the entire region are
in danger of falling to a Russian invasion.

The Carter administration, according to Henry Kissinger,
actually encourages revolutions which overthrow right-wing
dictators in the belief that "by demonstrating our moral values and concern for human rights we will gain the appropa-
tion of mankind and thus outflank the Soviets. But reality is
more complex.

"It is a hard fact that some societies whose security is vital
to us—particularly in the Persian Gulf—are governed by au-
thoritarian conservative regimes."

There was a lesson to be learned in the Iran situation,
Kissinger added. "Iran should teach us that humane values
are not necessarily served by the overthrow of conservative
regimes."[3]

Kissinger's statement could be applied not only to current situations but to the past as well—to China, to Cuba, to southeast Asia, Latin America and Africa.

This We Change—This We Don't

As I conclude this section, I would like to re-emphasize something which I reported in the preceeding chapter: Every U.S. Secretary of State since 1944, with the exception of James F. Byrnes, has been a member of the Council on Foreign Relations.

I believe that the historic record of this group's influence upon our foreign policy, with its unbroken string of defeats and accommodations to the communists, is appalling. The decline of the U.S.'s international position has occurred under this one organization's guidance.

Though presidents and political parties have changed, foreign policy has not. I believe it is high time for the citizens of this country to clean this "elite" group out of the Department of State and replace it with some people with common sense and courage.

These "leaders" have already given the communists our shirts; let's not let them give away our pants too.

CRISIS OF DEPENDABLE ALLIES

Our allies read the significance of America's foreign policy better than most American citizens do.

The abandonment of allies like the South Vietnamese, the Chinese of Taiwan and the Shah of Iran, combined with everything else I have discussed in this chapter, has produced a very shaky confidence in the U.S.

This was reflected recently by Qatar's leader, Sheik Khalifa bin Hamad of Thani. The U.S. had asked to put military bases in his Middle East country. The Sheik responded, "We don't trust Americans anymore. We don't know if the Americans are serious about stopping the Russians."[4]

NATO nations, particularly West Germany and France, are losing confidence in the U.S as an ally. Carter's reversal of his decision to deploy the neutron bomb in NATO countries is one reason for this loss of confidence.

Another reason is the U.S. acceptance of the Soviet demand that the "Backfire" bomber airplane and the SS-20 nuclear missile be excluded from the SALT arms limitation agreement. These two medium-range weapons pose a direct threat to western Europe's defensibility, and because they are not included in the SALT agreements, Russia can increase its arsenal of these weapon systems.

The NATO member countries are beginning to doubt the U.S. resolve to stay ahead of the Soviets militarily. They doubt even more America's willingness to make the sacrifices necessary to counter the Soviet arms buildup and communism's increasingly bold and aggressive expansionism.

Soon, western Europe may decide that the U.S. is worthless as an ally in the fight against communism. When that happens, the Europeans will make their own peace with the Soviets, leaving the U.S. isolated and vulnerable.

Pakistan's Snub

Just after the Soviets invaded Afghanistan, the U.S. rushed to Pakistan offering that nation a $400 million military aid package. Pakistani president General Mohammed Zia ul-Haq flatly rejected the offer.

"What do I buy with $400 million?" he asked. "The hostility of the Soviet Union, and that does not suit me."[5]

I'm sure he turned the offer down for one simple reason: He was uncertain that the U.S. would continue to support his country if the Russians decide to invade.

Our country's survival depends in great measure upon the faith of our allies in our resolve to stay strong and resolute when dealing with the communists.

But our foreign policy record doesn't engender a whole lot of faith. Neither does our current military strength, when compared with the Russian armed forces, inspire great security for our allies.

No country wants to stand with us against the Soviet Union today and then be left to fight the Russians alone tomorrow.

THE CRISIS OF INTERNAL DECAY

The Threat Of Self-Doubt

Many in America have begun to doubt the free enterprise system—in fact, every principle and system—which helped to make this a great nation.

Although no way is perfect, the democratic, capitalist free-enterprise system has produced more freedom, prosperity and financial independence for more people than any other system in history.

Yet a number of people in America have been traveling through a long period of self-doubt, criticizing the American way to the point where they ignore its great benefits and strengths.

The Threat Of The "Welfare State"

Since Franklin Roosevelt's "New Deal," a kind of "free lunch" mentality has begun working its way into the American mind.

Welfare programs, grown large because of recipients' attitudes and the self-perpetuating nature of the bureaucracies which run them, threaten to strangle the entire economy.

I say "strangle" because, since the government itself has no money, it must *take* from the taxpayer to *feed* the welfare system.

Although people who are truly needy should receive *some* help, the present system is riddled with loopholes. For instance, we allow families to stay on welfare for three generations and longer, in some cases. Children in these families are born *expecting* to be supported by the state.

An illustration of how welfare instills its own "giveaway" principles in people occurred in Pennsylvania recently.

There, Governor Richard Thornburgh proposed that 81,000 able-bodied welfare recipients be placed in state-supported jobs. The new program was dubbed "workfare."

There was an immediate uproar of protest against this plan. Local "welfare rights" groups staged sit-ins and demonstrations at welfare offices across the state. Mind you, this was not because welfare recipients would be tossed into economic peril, but because they would now have to *work* for their tax-supported paychecks.

Even state legislators, mostly from districts heavy with welfare recipients, attacked the bill, threatening to "filibuster" it to death.

The Bible On Work

There are some definite God-given Biblical principles which apply to this welfare situation.

Paul the Apostle wrote: "In the name of the Lord Jesus Christ, we command you, brothers, to keep away from every brother who is idle and does not live according to the teaching you received from us. For you yourselves know how you ought to follow our example. We were not idle when we were with you, nor did we eat anyone's food without paying for it. On the contrary, we worked night and day, laboring and toiling so that we would not be a burden to any of you.

"We did that, not because we do not have the right to such help (as God's Apostles), but in order to make ourselves a model for you to follow. For even when we were with you, we gave you this rule: 'If a man will not work, he shall not eat' " (2 Thessalonians 3:6–10 NIV).

One of our own system's greatest men, President Lincoln, set forth a maxim concerning a man's self-respect and freedom: "You never help a man when you do for him what he can and should do for himself." We seem to have forgotten his words.

The Threat Of Bureaucracy

All of the blame for the mess the welfare system is causing in our economy cannot fall on the recipients themselves. Much of it goes to the bureaucrats. In fact, a great deal of what is hurting our system is the *giant bureaucracy* we have built to run it.

A high government official recently charged that bureaucracies are discouraged from saving money. In fact, the system *encourages* them to *waste* it.

That's because a bureau manager's earnings, power and prestige all rest on how many people work under him and how much money his department spends. If he cuts either category, he cuts his own power.

One freshman senator was recently shocked by his first brush with a Washington bureau.

He learned that the bureau heads were in a panic because, nearing the end of the fiscal year, they still had several millions of unspent dollars in their budget.

Quickly, they found a way to spend the leftover funds.

The reason for their panic? Easy. If the bureaucrats turned the money in at the end of the fiscal year, their budget for the next year would be cut by that same amount.

So without the American people watching and keeping tabs, the giant governmental bureaucracies will never reduce their size. For them to do it themselves would be foolish; after all, we reward them with more money and more workers when they spend, and penalize them when they save.

Only the actions of courageous legislators can cut the waste our bureaucracies cause. But these lawmakers must act soon. We are burying ourselves beneath a greater and greater national debt each year.

The Threat Of Socialist Thinking

Can the government support us, or give us something for nothing? That's the principle behind socialism. But a government strong enough to support its citizens from the cradle to the grave also has the power to take their freedom away.

Freedom is not free—it is quite expensive.

Today, we are in a life-or-death contest with the totalitarian system of communism. If we can't build a credible deterrent to the growing Soviet military machine, then we will soon be taken over, and we will cease to exist as a free society. Then it won't matter who our allies are.

If anyone thinks it would be easier to surrender to the communists or the socialists than to make the sacrifices necessary to fight them, ask yourself this:

Why have thousands of eastern Europeans risked their lives trying to climb the Berlin Wall?

Why have tens of thousands of South Vietnamese left all their belongings behind and risked their lives on perilous waters in unseaworthy boats to leave communist Vietnam?

Why have Cambodians by the hundreds of thousands fled their own land to live in inadequate refugee camps in Thailand?

Why have thousands of Cubans abandoned all their possessions and risked their lives by seeking asylum at the Peruvian embassy in their own capital city of Havana?

All those people—Cubans, Germans, Asians, Russians and more have risked—and lost—their lives to escape communism. So why are so many Americans unwilling to sacrifice and risk even a little to prevent communism's spread?

Does Man Live By Bread Alone?

Man is far more than just a physical being, and he has more than physical needs. Man has always struggled and fought for personal freedom, which is a spiritual need.

Yet, throughout history, people who have been born into free societies have always taken that freedom for granted. They rarely think of the sacrifices that had to be made generations earlier to win that freedom.

Will today's Americans discover too late what a precious blessing from almighty God our freedom is? Our system, with all its flaws, still offers more freedom and opportunity for more people than any system ever to exist on the planet.

To conclude, let's turn to Italian socialist Franco Ferrarotti. He said: "Socialism might work if it were possible to invent a new man, but until then, capitalism has the advantage in inventiveness. The only thing that can kill capitalism is for it to slip into bureaucratic stagnation."[6]

Learn A Lesson From Foreign Investors

Our system needs some repairs, particularly in cutting the wastefulness of bureaucracy.

We also need a form of "compassionate capitalism." We need to help those who are truly needy.

But let's not lose sight of the overwhelming benefits of our free enterprise system. Foreign investors haven't. Listen to what Francois de Combret, an advisor to the president of France, has to say:

"Look at OPEC. They will still put most of their money in the U.S. There is nothing European investors want more than to invest in the U.S. The reason is your capitalist system. Your crisis is caused not by the system but by the workings of the system. When an engine breaks down, you don't call the principle of internal combustion into question. You fix or replace the engine."

I think that Frenchman has good advice for Americans. We need to clean house in Washington, and elect a Congress and a President who believe in the capitalist system.

Our Congress has been dominated and controlled since 1955 by men and women who don't really believe in capitalism. The President can recommend laws and execute policy, but Congress runs the country.

During the past 25 years, the majority in Congress has vastly increased the size of government and the size of its cost. They have plunged us deeper into debt.

At the same time, they have allowed our international standing to fall perilously, and our mighty military power to slip into second-class status. With no intention to be politically partisan, I think it's time to rid Congress of those of *any* party who consistently vote for big government and big spending. In the final analysis, some "leaders" don't really believe in—don't really want to sacrifice for—our free capitalist society.

CRISIS OF MILITARY WEAKNESS

Military power is such a critical area for the United States that it needs more discussion here, even though it has been dealt with in previous chapters. I want to start by looking at warfare in light of what the Bible teaches us.

A Christian View Of War

In the Sermon on the Mount (Matthew chapter 5), Jesus made many statements which have been jerked out of context and used to justify pacifism under any and all circumstances.

Though some sincere people with earnest motives have been honestly confused by this passage, I have run into many who confuse the issue for other motives.

Many of these people don't know or believe the rest of the Bible. But they cling to a few statements which they distort to justify their cause.

To understand this sermon, we must first know why Jesus preached it.

The religious leaders of his day, called Pharisees, had distorted the true meaning of the Law of Moses by adding their own traditions to it. So Jesus had to show them the original meaning of the law.

Thou Shalt Not Kill

Remember, though, Jesus did not *change* the law, he restored its original meaning. To have changed the meaning would have been saying that God had made a mistake, which is impossible because of His nature. With that in mind, let's look at the passages in dispute.

Jesus said, "You have heard that the ancients were told (referring to the religious tradition), 'You shall not commit murder' and 'Whoever commits murder shall be liable to the court' " (Matthew 5:21 NASB).

Both the original Hebrew in the Old Testament and the Greek in the New Testament say, "You shall not murder." But it is obvious that the Bible didn't mean *all* killing is wrong. After all, God commanded the Hebrews to stone a murderer to death.

In this part of His sermon, Jesus takes murder back to the motive and shows that even to call someone a fool, in the future kingdom of God will be considered grounds for capital punishment.

So, far from saying there should be no killing under any circumstances, He was making capital punishment applicable to motives *as well as* action.

An Eye for an Eye

Jesus later said, "You have heard that it was an eye for an eye and a tooth for a tooth. But I say to you, do not resist him who is evil; but whoever slaps you on your right cheek, turn to him the other also" (Matthew 5:38–39 NASB).

In this case, Jesus was citing the false application of a commandment of God by the religious leaders.

"An eye for an eye and a tooth for a tooth" comes from Exodus 21:22–25. That passage gave instructions to civil court judges on how to judge equitably—how to make the punishment fit the crime.

The religious leaders took this order and made it a principle of inter-personal relationships; they used it to justify revenge. They also neatly circumvented the most important of God's commandments—"You shall love your neighbor as yourself."

Instruction To Soldiers

When John the Baptist preached repentance, some soldiers asked him how they should live to remain consistent with their new faith.

John said, "Do not take money from anyone by force, or accuse anyone falsely, and be content with your wages" (Luke 3:14 NASB).

At that time, the Roman soldiers were known for supplementing their incomes by robbing people and taking bribes. John condemns that—not using force in the line of duty. He did not say "you must quit being soldiers in order to come into the faith."

Instructions About Legitimate Authority

God said through Paul the Apostle: "Let every person be in subjection to the governing authorities. For there is no authority except from God, and those which exist are established by God . . . for rulers are not a cause for fear for good behavior, but for evil. Do you want to have no fear of authority? Do what is good, and you will have praise from the same; for it is a minister of God to you for good. But if you do what is evil, be afraid; for it does not bear the *sword* for nothing; for it is a minister of God, an avenger who brings wrath upon the one who practices evil" (Romans 13:1–4 NASB).

There are several important principles contained here.

First, God ordained governments to keep order and peace and protect the property and person of their citizens.

Second, God ordained the officer with the sword (or a gun today) to enforce the law—to protect the innocent and punish the guilty.

From this belief comes a larger application. If a nation (or an individual) seeks to take away the life, liberty and property of another, then that government or person is to be punished by force.

If a police officer chasing a criminal were to "turn the other cheek," he would have his head blown off. If a nation turned the other cheek to a Hitler or a Brezhnev, it would be conquered. And freedom for all men would die.

In a world of fallen men, peace, security and freedom can only be maintained by power strong enough to discourage those bent upon conquest. The stronger a nation's military, the less likely it is that it will ever have to fight.

That's why I believe that the Bible supports building a powerful military force. And the Bible is telling the U.S. to become strong again. A weak military will encourage the Soviet Union to start an all-out war.

Let us now discuss the present situation. Henry Kissinger, former Secretary of State, has warned us: "It (the balance of military power) is shifting so rapidly against the U.S. that in a future confrontation like that with Cuba in 1962 or the Mideast alert in 1973, it will be the Soviet Union which will possess the quantitative superiority in strategic weapons."[7] (The term "strategic weapons" refers to nuclear warheads and the systems which deliver them. This also includes systems which defend against nuclear attack.)

Why More Nukes?

Some people ask, "Why does the U.S. need more strategic weapons when we already have so many?"

The reason is that we face a determined enemy—the Soviet Union—which has demonstrated since World War II that it is totally committed to becoming the most powerful military power on Earth.

Even when the U.S. had a clear superiority over the U.S.S.R. in terms of military strength, we allowed the Soviets to catch up in hopes of putting an end to the arms race.

But the Russians took advantage of our desire to agree on the Strategic Arms Limitation Treaty (SALT) and passed us in nuclear capabilities.

A Clear Lead

Now the Russians have the clear edge, not only in numbers of strategic weapons but in the explosive power of each warhead.

Secretary of Defense Dr. Harold Brown recently testified: "The Soviets are deploying the SS-18 and SS-19 (missiles) in such numbers that they will have high assurance of destroying the bulk of Minutemen (largest U.S. missile) silos in a pre-emptive strike in the early 1980s."[8]

Let me translate. That means that the Soviet SS-18 missile can hit any target in the U.S. with such accuracy that the most it could miss by would be 400 yards. Some of those SS-18 missiles carry 100-megaton warheads (I explained the damage those warheads can do in chapter 6).

These same missiles can also carry three 25-megaton warheads, each independently targeted. That means that one missile could drop deadly warheads on three different cities. New York, Philadelphia and Washington, D.C. could be vaporized by one of these missiles.

The SS-18 can even carry 10 one-magaton warheads, each with a different destination. And a one-megaton warhead is capable of destroying a major city. (One megaton is equal to 50 Hiroshima-sized bombs.)

The Soviet SS-19 missile is only slightly less lethal. It carries six independently-targeted one-megaton warheads. The Soviets also have several types of smaller missiles which are not included in the SALT agreement. These can be converted into long-range killers capable of hitting targets in the U.S. All they have to do is add another rocket booster to their SS-20 missile and it can hit the U.S.

The U.S. has nothing to compare with the SS-18 and SS-19 missiles. Our largest missile can carry only three one-megaton warheads.

No Way To Verify

There is no way for the U.S. to know exactly how many nuclear warheads the Soviets have. Nor can we determine how many additional rocket boosters they may have hidden away to add to their SS-20 missiles.

The SALT agreement is based on the Soviets' honestly giving their word about what weapons they possess—and you know what the Soviets' word is worth.

Major General John K. Singlaub, former chief of staff of U.S. forces in Korea, gives his opinion of the honesty of the Russian leaders: "From a historical point of view, it's clear that we cannot trust the Soviets to keep SALT II. Out of 27 summit agreements with the Soviets, they have broken or cheated on all but one. And that includes SALT I."[9]

The First Strike Threat

Part of the clear and apparent danger Defense Secretary Brown referred to earlier in this chapter is the Soviet Union's ability to destroy our missiles in a "first strike"—a surprise attack.

Since the U.S. has considerably less missiles than the U.S.S.R. does, and even less warheads with great destructive power, we are now in an extremely dangerous situation.

The danger is spelled out in a book prepared by a blue-ribbon panel of military experts and members of Congress.

The book, titled *An Analysis of SALT II*, contends: "In short, the Soviets will soon have a 'first-strike capability' authorized by SALT. And when that capability is in hand, Soviet leaders may logically presume that the U.S. would not retaliate after a first strike.

"Soviet leaders could reason that a U.S. President would not order a retaliation, knowing that his *few* surviving weapons could not annihilate the Soviet society; and that a counterstrike by Soviet second-strike weapons would, in fact, utterly destroy the U.S. as a viable society.

"The fact is that after a first strike, *the Soviets would have more missiles and bombers in reserve for the second strike than the U.S. had to start with.*"[10]

Are the Soviets preparing to launch a first strike? All of the latest intelligence on the numbers and types of weapons the U.S.S.R. is acquiring say the Soviets want the power to be able to mount such an attack.

Here is the evidence:

• The U.S.S.R. has a vast superiority in warheads of the large sizes.

• The Soviets have great numbers of submarine-launched ballistic missiles (SLBMs) which can hit the U.S. from as far away as the Bering Sea. U.S. SLBMs have a maximum range of 2,500 miles, and they carry smaller warheads than the Russian variety.

• The U.S.S.R. has built up a superior bomber fleet, many of which are of the new "Backfire" type, which can hit the U.S. and then land in Cuba. An extra aid for Soviet planes was recently reported: "Air Force experts say U.S. air defenses are so porous that the Soviet Union could sneak as many as 50 bombers through gaps in the radar net for a surprise attack on key command centers."[11]

(A related shock was announced recently. An article in *U.S. News and World Report* revealed the deficiencies of the U.S. fighter planes that would be used to intercept Soviet bombers. The article said: "Besides engine problems, the F-14, F-15 and F-16 have also been hit by shortages of spare parts, which U.S. Representative Jack Edwards (R-Ala.) claims are grounding half the planes.")[12]

• The Soviets have built up numbers of SS-5 anti-aircraft and anti-ICBM missiles, which can strike up to 150,000 feet with a range of 200 miles. This buildup occurred in direct violation of the SALT agreement (the U.S. has dismantled its anti-missile system, as it agreed to do). See exhibit V.

• The Soviets have developed a massive civil defense system of elaborate shelters. One estimate says that most of the Soviet population could survive a nuclear strike in these shelters. This is a specific violation of the SALT pact, which says there can be no civil defense system (the U.S. has abided by this part of the agreement to the letter). See exhibit VI.

• The U.S.S.R. has developed and deployed satellites with laser-beam missile attackers. These satellites can destroy any U.S. missile that might survive a Soviet first strike.

What Are The Soviets Up To?

In light of the present Soviet military strength and that nation's obvious efforts to become even stronger the question comes up: What are the Soviet intentions?

It's obvious what the Soviets do *not* intend to do. While the U.S. has used restraint and not even built weapon levels up to the limits imposed by SALT I, the Soviets have gone beyond the allowed numbers of warheads, missiles and so on. We know they have cheated.

SALT Hurts

A group of military experts recently assessed the U.S.S.R.'s intentions this way:

"Soviet strategic doctrine is not based on deterrence and the presumption that nuclear war is unwinnable. To the contrary, Soviet doctrine holds that nuclear war can be fought and won, if the Soviet Union takes full advantage of the effects of surprise attack.

"Soviet ICBMs reflect this doctrine in both size and number of warheads. They have been designed to destroy the American missile force.

"The Soviet emphasis on defensive measures, especially the hardening of their ICBM silos, also indicates their assumption that nuclear war is neither impossible nor unwinnable.

"The SALT process has in no way worked to encourage the Soviets to adopt a strategy of defense rather than offense. Indeed, the special grant to the Soviet Union in both SALT I and SALT II of large numbers of heavy ICBMs has specifically emboldened them to embrace the strategy of first strike (surprise attack)."[13]

It's Time to Pass the SALT

While the Soviets have been increasing their nuclear potential, the U.S. has been doing quite the opposite.

The U.S.S.R. has shown the world that it means to win the

nuclear war that may someday come to pass; the U.S. has shown the world that it does not want to even *think* about winning that war.

The point of the SALT agreements was to ensure that neither country would have the potential to wipe out the other's total nuclear arsenal with a first strike. That condition would then deter either country from attacking, since it could not do so without being attacked itself. Neither side was to build anti-missile systems or civilian defense programs, so each country's people would be, in effect, the other country's hostages.·

The U.S. has held to the spirit and the letter of SALT. The Soviets have not. For that reason, we find ourselves at this incredible disadvantage.

SALT is finished. There's no more basis for negotiation. It is time to use our vast and superior technology to create the world's strongest military power. Only this will stop the Soviets' insane rush toward nuclear war.

A President's Dilemma

If something isn't done quickly, the Soviet Premier may soon telephone the American President. The Premier will say: "We can destroy your missile silos.

"We can intercept and destroy all incoming submarine launched missiles with our laser beams.

"We can destroy your obsolete bombers with our MIG-25 fighters and SS-5 ground-to-air missiles.

"So, Mr. President, will you surrender? Or shall we destroy your country? You have 20 seconds to decide."

What would you advise the President to do at that moment? Let's get tough and not let that moment happen.

Our Endangered Oil "Life Line"

The map on the following page shows the routes followed by the tankers which bring us the bulk of our imported oil supplies. There is no OTHER way that our oil supply can be delivered to us from the Middle East. The shaded areas of the

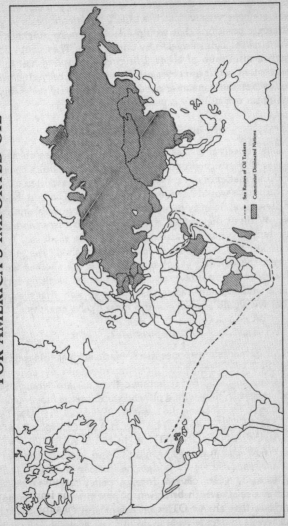

VITAL SEA LANES
FOR AMERICA'S IMPORTED OIL

----- Sea Routes of Oil Tankers

///// Communist Dominated Nations

map reflect Soviet dominated countries. As you can see, the Soviets have wisely "patch-worked" their conquests to gain strategic positions that would enable them to quickly close the vital sea lanes traveled by our tankers. They could do so with a minimum of effort, bringing a complete halt to the movement of our imported oil. This oil is not only vital to our industrial and consumer needs, it is absolutely necessary to maintain our military capabilities.

If Our Sea Lanes Were Closed

It is conceivable that if the Russians did close these sea lanes, our entire economy and democracy could collapse within a matter of days. Without the flow of imported oil, the government would have to put an emergency ban on the sale of diesel fuel in order to reserve that fuel for possible military use. Without diesel fuel, the trucks which carry food from our farms to our cities would not be able to do so. If the population of the cities panicked and "rushed" the grocery stores, the existing supplies of food on the shelves would disappear within a few days in most cities. Nothing incites chaos and anarchy faster than hunger, and that's exactly what we would see—chaos and most likely, anarchy.

Impossible?

Our immediate response to a scenario such as this is one of unbelief. We think, "our government would never let the Russians do that." But remember, the Russians wouldn't be declaring war, they would only be stopping the movement of petroleum by blocking the sea lanes. WOULD THE UNITED STATES BE THE FIRST TO LAUNCH A NUCLEAR ATTACK AGAINST A NATION WITH WHICH WE ARE NOT EVEN AT WAR? Of course we wouldn't. And nothing short of a nuclear response would budge the Russian blockade. Judging from 30 years of past foreign policy, and the lack of prompt decisive military action in past times, one can only conclude that an American president and Congress would take weeks to decide what to do . . . and every nation in the world including Russia KNOWS that this would be precisely how we would respond.

SOME HOPE FROM ANOTHER POWER

If you are a Christian reading this book, then it is up to you to get involved in preserving this country. True, the Lord could come at any moment, but we may go through some terrible trials before He comes for us.

We should plan our lives as though we will live them out fully. But we should live each day with the idea: "Jesus could come today." That means that we must actively take on the responsibility of being a citizen and a member of God's family.

We need to get active electing officials who will not only reflect the Bible's morality in government but will shape domestic and foreign policies to protect our country and our way of life.

We need to elect men and women who will have the courage to make the tough decisions needed to insure our nation's survival. They must be willing to clamp down on big government, cut exploitation of the welfare system, keep our strong commitments to our allies and stand up to communist expansion.

We need people who see how important a strong military is to keeping peace for us and what remains of the free world.

The More Important Duty

I believe there are four main reasons why the U.S. has been preserved as a free country.

The *first* reason is that this country is made up of a large community of true believers in the Lord Jesus Christ. God has spared many nations in the past because they had experienced spiritual awakenings. We have enjoyed a spiritual awakening in the U.S. over the past few years. We must keep evangelism moving.

The *second* reason is that the U.S. has supported and provided for missionaries who take the message of salvation out across the world. We must increase our support.

The *third* reason is that the U.S. has stood behind Jews and the nation of Israel in their times of need. Both here and in the Middle East, we have fought persecution of the Jewish people and their nation, many times when no one else would help. God said to Abraham, the father of all Jews: "I'll bless those who bless you, and I will curse those who curse you."

This promise was extended to protect all the descendents of Abraham, Isaac and Jacob (Genesis 12:3 and 27:29). I believe that if the U.S. ever turns its back on Israel, we will no longer exist as a nation. Don't take this lightly, for throughout history the rise and fall of empires can be directly related to how they treated the Jews.

The *fourth* reason the U.S. stands strong is that God's people pray. But as we have seen, it is time to mount a massive bombardment of God's throne with prayers for our nation and our leaders.

God spoke about what he would do for a nation in a situation like ours today: "If my people, who are called by my name, shall humble themselves and turn from their wicked ways, and seek my face, then I will hear from heaven, and I will heal their land."

I believe that America will survive this perilous situation and endure until the Lord comes to evacuate His people. But this will only be because God's people have humbled themselves, turned from their sins in repentence and sought God's face in prayer.

Let us get about the business of prayer to preserve this nation.

ELEVEN
LESSON FROM A FIG TREE

"Now learn this lesson from the fig tree: As soon as its twigs get tender and its leaves come out, you know that summer is near. Even so, when you see all these things (the prophecies being fulfilled), you know that it is near, right at the door. I will tell you the truth, this generation will certainly not pass away until all these things have happened."

—Jesus of Nazareth
(Matthew 24:32–34 NIV)

Even if I didn't know anything about prophecy, I would know enough from studying what is going on in our world to see that we are headed toward catastrophe.

As previously was quoted, Dr. George Wald, the Nobel Prize-winning scientist, said, "I am one of those scientists who finds it hard to see how the human race is to bring itself much past the year 2000."

"Where will all this lead?" "Will there be a nuclear holocaust?" "Is there any hope for me, personally?" In light of so many perils we face, questions like these come to mind.

Shortly before Jesus was crucified, He predicted the destruction of Jerusalem. After He spoke, His disciples asked *Him* some urgent questions.

They asked, "Tell us when will this happen, and what will be the sign of Your coming and of the end of the age?" (Matthew 24:3)

Jesus answered their questions with many predictions about the world conditions and signs that would herald His return and the end of history as we know it. We have studied many of these prophecies in this book.

After Jesus announced His many signs, He paused. Then He told a parable that applied to all that had been taught.

161

THE FIG TREE

Jesus said, "Now learn the parable from the fig tree: When its branch has become tender, and puts forth its leaves, you know that summer is near . . ." (Matthew 24:32 NASB).

A parable is a method of teaching that was popular with Jesus. Parables are stories which teach, usually communicating one important point.

The obvious point of Jesus' fig tree parable is to teach us to identify a "general time period." When the tree's leaves first begin to bud, we know that summer is near.

This is still true in Israel today. I've seen the fig tree leaves begin to bud there. I once asked an Israeli friend what that budding meant. He immediately replied, "It's springtime, and summer is coming."

After completing the parable, Jesus connected its figurative meaning to the point He was trying to make: "Even so," He said, "You too, when you see all these things (all the prophecies coming together), recognize that it is near, right at the door" (Matthew 24:33 NASB).

Jesus made the connection for us. Just as we know that summer is near when we see the fig leaves first appear, so can we know that the end of history and Jesus's return are near by the simultaneous appearance of all His predicted signs.

Then Jesus told us the point of the parable: "Truly I say to you, this generation will not pass away until all these things take place" (Matthew 24:34 NASB).

But what generation was Jesus talking about? In the context of His words on the signs, He could only have meant the generation that would see all the prophetic predictions come together. The generation that witnesses that coming-together will not pass away until all things predicted come to pass.

WE ARE THE GENERATION HE WAS TALKING ABOUT! I say that because, unmistakably, for the first time in history, all the signs are coming together at an accelerating rate.

What do I mean? Look around you and see:

• Earthquakes are increasing in frequency; the greatest period for quakes in history is forecast for 1982.

• Famine spreads as population explodes.

• Pollution threatens our survival.

• Israel has been miraculously reborn as a nation.

• The U.S. is fading as a superpower.

• The Red Chinese continue to build their awesome army.

• Arabs and all the world's Moslems threaten a war that would destroy the State of Israel.

• All the world's powers appear ready to involve themselves in a Middle East war because of their need for oil.

• The European community of 10 grows stronger and begins to doubt the effectiveness of the U.S. as an ally.

• Nuclear holocaust seems more possible every day.

All these signs, and many more which are just as visible, point to the fact that this generation is the one that will see the end of the present world and the return of Jesus Christ.

Jesus went on to say, "No one knows the day or the hour" of His return. But he tells us how to "recognize" the generation during which He would come. We won't know the exact day or hour, He said, but we can know the general time.

"WHAT HOPE IS THERE?"

Some of you may have become distressed and frightened while reading this book. What hope is there, you may be asking. How did the world get into such a mess? Why can't men live with each other in peace? Why is history strewn with one case after another of man's inhumanity to man? Why can't I always do the things I know that I ought to do? Why can't children get along with parents, or husbands and wives get along without conflict?

I think we can see what the problem is: There's some kind

of malfunction in man himself. Historically, there have been many attempts to diagnose what the problem is.

The athiest Marxists say that man's basic problem is that he is corrupted by capitalism and the concepts of private property and competition that go along with it. They say the solution is to change man's environment and rid the world of corrupting influences.

But no communist society which has tried this solution can point to an example of a "new man." The age-old problems of greed, selfishness and cruelty are evident in communist countries too.

Much of the 20th century's agnostic philosophy has diagnosed man's basic problem as being a lack of education, culture and direction.

But Hitler's Germany blew that theory. There were more educated and cultured people living under the Third Reich than any nation in history.

The great Oxford University scholar C.S. Lewis summed up the failure of this diagnosis: "History demonstrates that education has only made man a more *clever* devil."

The great religions of history which assume that man is more than just a physical product of chance plus time (as evolution says) have also sought to change man's nature. They have introduced moral laws and teachings intended to show man the right way to live.

All these religions—except for one—state that man can make himself acceptable to God if he will just try to live by a moral code of behavior.

But that one exception is a unique and different religion. This religion has offered man two ways to approach God. We will call these approaches Plan A and Plan B.

PLAN A

Under Plan A, man assumes that he can do something to earn God's forgiveness and acceptance. To this man God holds out the Law of Moses and says to keep it. But because God is perfect, the standard is perfection.

The Bible says, "Whoever keeps the whole law and yet stumbles at just one point is guilty of breaking the whole law" (James 2:10 NIV).

Jesus further explained the meaning of this approach to the religious leaders of his day. They said that God accepted them because they had kept God's law.

Jesus said that if a man looked after a woman with lust in his heart, then he had committed adultery. He also said that if a man hates his brother and calls him an empty-headed fool, then that man is guilty of murder (Matthew 5:21–31).

In other words, Jesus showed that in God's eyes, thinking about doing something is the same as doing it. That's why no man has ever succeeded in reaching God through this approach. It requires *total* moral perfection. But it is a way that is offered, if you would like to try (good luck).

PLAN B

That leaves us Plan B. This plan is what makes the Judeo-Christian Bible unique.

All other religions say that man must do something or live up to a standard in order to earn God's acceptance. Plan B says that you must start your approach to God by admitting that you *can't* offer anything that God, in His perfection, can accept.

Solomon was the king of Israel whom God inspired to write the Book of Proverbs. A long time ago, Solomon found that he could never make it to God by keeping His law.

Solomon said, "Indeed there is not a righteous man on Earth who continually does good and who never sins" (Ecclesiastes 7:20 NASB).

The prophet Isaiah said much the same thing 750 years before Christ. In God's sight, he said, "we all have become

like one who is unclean, and all of our righteous deeds are
like filthy garments" (Isaiah 64:6).

Is there a solution? Back in the Old Testament era, God
gave man a temporary way to approach Him. This way was
used long before the Law of Moses was given.

The Temporary Solution

God gave man the animal sacrifice system in order to teach
him the ultimate solution. Under this system, men would
confess their sins and then sacrifice a spotless lamb to God.
This was to teach man that an innocent substitute of God's
choice had to pay for the sins of the world.

When God handed down the Law of Moses, the animal
sacrifice system was made even more specific. This was to
show that, from the very beginning, God knew man could
never keep the new Laws. For if he could, why would God
have given the animal sacrifice system?

Obviously, animal sacrifice couldn't offer a permanent forgiveness for sins. Sacrifices had to be performed continually,
thus showing that they were merely a temporary solution,
and that a better way would soon come.

A Messiah Opens the Way

Plan B offered that better way. Isaiah predicted the new
way centuries before it came. He spoke of the Messiah-
Savior that God would send to open the way to Him. Isaiah
said that this Messiah would be rejected by his own people,
and that the Jewish nation would not believe the message
about the Messiah (Isaiah 53:1–3).

Then, more than seven centuries before it happened,
Isaiah gave a vivid description of how God would remove
man's sin and make it possible for man to gain fellowship
with Him.

Isaiah's Incredible Vision

Isaiah predicted: "Surely our griefs He Himself (the Messiah) bore, and our sorrows He carried; yet we ourselves
esteemed Him stricken, smitten of God.

"But He was wounded for our transgressions, He was crushed for our iniquities; the chastening for our peace fell upon Him, and by His scourging we are healed. All of us like sheep have gone astray, each of us has turned to his own way; but the Lord has caused the iniquity of us all to fall upon Him.

"He was oppressed and He was afflicted, yet He did not open His mouth (to defend Himself); like a lamb that is led to slaughter, and like a sheep that is silent before its shearers, so He did not open His mouth.

"By oppression and violence He was taken away; and as for His generation (race), who considered that He was cut off out of the land of the living, for the transgression of my (Isaiah's) people to whom the stroke was due?" (Isaiah 53:4–8 NASB).

This amazing prophecy shows many things.

First, Isaiah predicts that God would put man's sins, previously borne by animals, upon the Messiah. He then clearly says that the Messiah would be judged in our place for our transgressions of God's laws.

Second, Isaiah says that the judgement of the Messiah would heal us from our sins.

Finally, Isaiah predicted that the Jewish nation, at least for the most part, would reject the Messiah and accuse Him of being "smitten" of God.

The Galilean Candidate

There has been only one Jew in history who fit Isaiah's description, and that was none other than the carpenter from Nazareth, Jesus.

When the prophet John the Baptist was illumined by God that Jesus was the promised Messiah, he exclaimed, "Behold the lamb of God who takes away the sin of the world" (John 1:29). John immediately related Jesus to the Messiah's mission revealed in Isaiah's prophecy.

Jesus Himself announced that His ultimate purpose was to fulfill Isaiah's prophecy when He said: "For even the Son of

Man did not come to be served, but to serve, and to give His life a ransom for many."

HOW AND WHY PLAN B WORKS

Here's what makes Plan B work. The Bible says, "God made Him (Jesus) who had no sin to be sin for us, so that in Him we might become the righteousness of God" (2 Corinthians 5:21 NIV).

Since Jesus the Messiah lived a perfect life, He qualified to pay for the sins of others. So God took all our sins and put them on Jesus. Then He judged the Messiah in our place.

When we believe this, God exchanges the guilt of our sins for Jesus's righteousness. He actually clothes us with the perfect righteousness of the Messiah. At that moment, we become forever acceptable to the perfect and holy God.

A New Nature

The moment we ask Jesus the Messiah into our lives, several things happen.

The first thing is that we are miraculously given a new spiritual dimension of life. This new dimension possesses God's own nature. With it, we can understand and know God and His Word. We begin to desire the things that please God. This is known as being "born again" (see John Chapter 3).

A New Power

A second thing that happens is that God's Spirit takes up permanent residence inside of us. We have a new source of power to become different, and God begins to change us from the inside.

This new power is what makes Plan B—and Christianity—so different from other religions and their teachings. All other religions depend on man's ability to change himself. Those religions can clean up man's outside, but not his heart.

Jesus Christ comes into our hearts through the Holy Spirit and begins to change us. He gives us new desires and the power to satisfy them. This kind of change—from the inside instead of the outside—is revolutionary.

A New Purpose

I used to think it would be a real drag to become a follower of Jesus. The few exposures that I had to churches made me think I would have to make a list of the 10 things I really loved and give them up and then make a list of the 10 things I hated and start doing them.

This isn't how it works at all. The change takes place on the *inside*, in our hearts and motives. And it doesn't happen all at once: It is a process of time. We find ourselves with a new purpose in life because God has shown us new values based on a new hope.

As we begin to realize that we have a certain and eternal destiny with God, our thinking about what's most important in this life begins to change.

A New Hope

As we see the prophecies that tell us that the world is heading toward a holocaust being fulfilled, we need a hope for right now. Besides helping us prepare for that final great catastrophe, we need hope to aid us in dealing with the world's *current* sad shape.

When we receive God's forgiveness through Plan B, we also get an incredible bonus—a "super-hope."

I realize that what I'm about to say will be difficult for some of you readers to believe. But I feel sure that Christ is coming very soon. The same prophets who have been 100 percent accurate about events in the past make this prediction about Christ's return. My belief is also backed by the personal promise of Jesus to those who believe in Him.

THE COMING COSMIC MYSTERY

The Apostle Paul said: "Listen, I tell you a mystery: We shall not all sleep (a Christian symbol for death), but we shall all be changed—in a flash, in the twinkling of an eye, the dead will be raised imperishable, and we (those who are still alive) shall be changed. For the perishable must clothe itself with the imperishable, and the mortal with immortality" (1 Corinthians 15:51–53 NIV).

The same "mystery" is further described in another passage: "According to the Lord's own word, we tell you that we who are still alive, who are left 'till the coming of the Lord, will certainly not precede those who have fallen asleep.

"For the Lord Himself will come down from heaven, with a loud command, with the voice of the archangel and with the trumpet call of God, and the dead in Christ will rise first. After that, we who are still alive and are left will be caught up with them in the clouds to meet the Lord in the air. And so we will be with the Lord forever. Therefore encourage each other with these words" (1 Thessalonians 4:15–18 NIV).

Unraveling the Mystery

Here's what these two prophecies mean: First, there is a time coming, and I believe absolutely that time will be during this generation, when suddenly and without warning, every true believer in Jesus will disappear from the Earth. That event's speed and suddenness will leave the nonbelieving world mystified.

Second, the believer is promised that, when this happens, he will be caught up to meet the Lord in the air.

And third, on the instantaneous trip upward to meet the Lord Jesus, all believers will be changed from mortal to immortal. This transformation was the main point of the mystery Paul was explaining.

The idea of being raised from the dead is familiar in the Old Testament. But Paul gave an entirely new promise here, one which stated that the generation alive when the Messiah returned would be changed from mortal to immortal without ever dying. We are the generation that will experience this incredible event.

When Does the Mystery Occur?

The really exciting aspect of this new hope is the time at which it occurs in relation to the prophetic timetable of events. If you look at exhibit VIII, you will see that there are two phases to Jesus's second coming.

The first phase, which we have discussed here, is commonly called "the Rapture." The second phase will come at the end of the most terrible period of history, which will last for seven years. It will be in this period that all the dreadful events predicted for the end-times will take place. This period is known as "the Tribulation."

After studying this issue for 25 years, I agree with many scholars in prophecy who say that the Rapture will occur *before* the Tribulation.

This is why the Apostle Paul told us to "comfort one another with these words." The incredible promise is that we will not be here on Earth when the horrible events we see shaping up before our eyes take place.

Where will the believers be when the world is going through its period of near-total destruction? Jesus said, "Do not let your heart be troubled. Trust in God, trust also in Me. There are many rooms in my Father's house; otherwise, I would have told you. I am going there to prepare a place for you. And if I go and prepare a place for you, I will come back and take you to be with me that you also may be where I am" (John 14:1–3 NIV).

THE PERSONAL RETURN

At the end of the seven-year Tribulation, when man is on the brink of annihilation in an all-out war, Jesus the Messiah will personally return and stop it. And all of us who believe now will return with Him in glorified bodies.

EXHIBIT VIII

PROPHETIC OUTLINE OF HISTORY

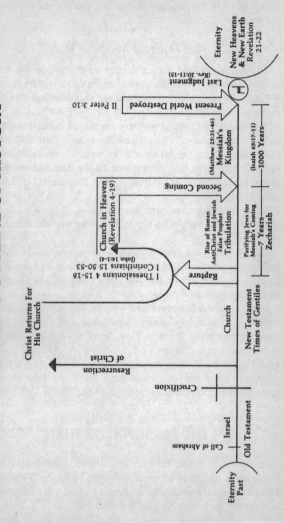

Utopia At Last

Jesus will then judge the survivors of the Tribulation period (see Matthew 25:31–46). Those who have believed in God's Messiah-Savior during the Tribulation will go as mortals into a new Earth and will repopulate it. It is then that all man's dreams of utopia will finally be realized (read Isaiah chapter 11 and chapter 65, verses 17–25).

This beginning period of the new world will last for 1,000 years. It will be during that period that the lines from Scripture which have been carved on the United Nations building in New York will be fulfilled. Those lines say: "They shall beat their swords into plowshares and their spears into pruning hooks. Nation will not lift up sword against nation, and never again will they ever learn war" (Isaiah 2:4 NASB).

THE AGE OF PEACE

The reason the above prophecy will come to pass is because the Prince of Peace Himself will rule the world. At last there will be a leader who cannot be corrupted by selfishness and the lust for power. Listen to what the Messiah, the Son of David, God's anointed king will do:

> "Then a shoot will spring from the stem of Jesse (Jesse was the father of King David. The 'shoot' refers to the Son of David, the Messiah).
> And a branch from his roots will bear fruit.
> And the Spirit of the Lord will rest on Him.
> The Spirit of wisdom and understanding,
>   the Spirit of counsel and strength,
>   the Spirit of knowledge and of reverence for the Lord.
> And He will delight in the fear of the Lord,
>   and He will not judge by what His eyes see,
>   nor make a decision by what His ears hear;
> But with righteousness He will judge the poor, and
>   decide with fairness for the afflicted of the earth.

"They will not hurt or destroy in all My holy mountain
(kingdom), for the earth will be full of the knowledge
of the Lord as waters cover the sea" (Isaiah 11:1–9).

This and many other prophecies speak of a one-world government that will finally work. But the one condition it requires
is clear: It will only work when the Messiah runs it.

A TIME TO CLAIM

The most important issue is, where do you stand? Do you
know that you are a forgiven person? Do you know that God is
real and that Jesus lives in you? Do you know where you are
going?

The choice is yours. You can change your eternal destiny
right now. You can know with certainty the answer to all the
questions I have just asked.

As I have shown previously in this chapter, God has dealt
with the sin barrier that keeps us from enjoying a personal
relationship with Him. But you must receive the pardon which
Jesus purchased for you, or the pardon is not yours. The question is, how can you receive this pardon?

The Bible says, "Yet to all who received Him (Jesus), who
believe in His name, He gave the right to become children of
God" (John 1:12 NIV). We receive Jesus and His pardon with a
simple prayer. It is so simple, in fact, that some people stumble
over it without knowing. All you need do is express to God that
in your heart the following things are true:

First, tell God that you know you have fallen short of His
perfect standards.

Then ask Him to forgive your sins because of what Jesus did
for you.

Finally, tell God you want Jesus to come into your life and
change it according to His plan. (I must say here that God
doesn't expect you to clean up your life; that's His job. He only
wants you to be willing for Him to do it.)

If you have prayed the prayer I just outlined, I want to be the first to congratulate you. You have just changed your eternal destiny. You now have Jesus the Messiah living inside you. God promised this, and He can't lie. Don't rely on an emotional reaction to tell you that you have changed. You may experience many emotions, but they will not be proof of the change.

And after you have prayed, don't sit there wondering if you were sincere enough, or if you had enough faith. The Bible says, "Whosoever shall call upon the name of the Lord shall be saved" (Romans 10:13). Just having considered God's offer and deciding that you wanted His plan for your life is all the proof of sincerity He requires.

SEE YOU SOON

It is my prayer that you have made the decision to accept the Lord. Also, I pray that you will carefully seek out other believers who follow the Bible. You will need to grow in your understanding of God's word.

We may go through a period of severe difficulty here in America before the Rapture comes. We need to be trained in how to believe God's promises and receive guidance and strength from Him.

I sincerely hope to see all who read this book at the soon-coming "family reunion."

Hal Lindsey
April 26, 1980

FOOTNOTES

Chapter 3
1. Douglas MacArthur, *Reminiscences* (McGraw-Hill: New York, 1964)

Chapter 4
1. Sarasota *Herald-Tribune*, Jan. 11, 1980

Chapter 5
1. Los Angeles *Times*, Oct. 25, 1974
2. *Newsweek*, Feb. 4, 1980
3. *The Bulletin* (Phila.), April 8, 1980
4. *Newsweek*, March 3, 1980
5. Ibid.
6. *Time*, Feb. 11, 1980
7. *Time*, Dec. 10, 1979
8. *Time*, Jan. 21, 1980

Chapter 6
1. Barry Goldwater, *With No Apologies* (William Morrow and Co.: New York, 1979)
2. *Time*, Feb. 18, 1980
3. *Time*, Jan. 28, 1980
4. Barry Goldwater, *With No Apologies* (William Morrow and Co.: New York, 1979)
5. *Time*, Feb. 18, 1980
6. *The Bulletin* (Phila.), March 30, 1980

Chapter 7
1. Douglas MacArthur, *Reminiscences* (McGraw-Hill: New York, 1964)
2. *Time*, Feb. 18, 1980
3. Ibid.

Chapter 8
1. *Time*, July 4, 1979
2. *U.S. News and World Report*, June 11, 1979

3. *Time*, June 11, 1979
4. Los Angeles *Times*, Feb. 4, 1980
5. *Newsweek*, June 11, 1979
6. *Aviation Week and Space Technology*, Nov. 26, 1979

Chapter 9

1. *America*, Feb. 5, 1977
2. *Newsweek*, June 16, 1975
3. Barry Goldwater, *With No Apologies* (William Morrow and Co.: New York, 1979)
4. *America*, Feb. 5, 1977
5. Ibid.
6. Ibid.
7. *Atlantic Monthly*, July, 1977
8. *U.S. News and World Report*, Feb. 21, 1977
9. Ibid.
10. *Christian Science Monitor*, Feb. 7, 1977
11. Barry Goldwater, *With No Apologies* (William Morrow and Co.: New York, 1979)
12. Ibid.

Chapter 10

1. *Time*, April 21, 1980
2. Barry Goldwater, *With No Apologies* (William Morrow and Co.: New York, 1979)
3. *Time*, April 21, 1980
4. *Newsweek*, Feb. 4, 1980
5. *Time*, March 24, 1980
6. *Time*, April 21, 1980
7. Ibid
8. The Coalition for Peace Through Strength, *An Analysis of SALT II*, 1979
9. Film, "The SALT Syndrome," produced by the Coalition for Peace Through Strength, 499 S. Capitol St., Washington, D.C. 20003, 1979
10. The Coalition for Peace Through Strength, *An Analysis of SALT II*, 1979
11. *U.S. News and World Report*, April 7, 1980
12. Ibid.
13. The Coalition for Peace Through Strength, *An Analysis of SALT II*, 1979

ABOUT THE AUTHOR

Hal Lindsey, named *the bestselling author of the decade* by the New York Times, was born in Houston, Texas. His first book, *The Late Great Planet Earth*, published in 1970, became the bestselling non-fiction book of the decade, selling more than 18 million copies worldwide. He is one of the few authors to have three books on the New York Times bestseller list at the same time.

Mr. Lindsey was educated at the University of Houston. After serving in the U.S. Coast Guard during the Korean War, Mr. Lindsey graduated from Dallas Theological Seminary where he majored in the New Testament and early Greek literature. After completing seminary, Mr. Lindsey served for eight years on the staff of Campus Crusade for Christ, speaking to tens of thousands of students on major university campuses throughout the United States.

Wayne Coombs Agency
75 Malaga Cove Plaza
Palos Verdes Estates, CA 90274
(213) 377-0420